ONLY ONE LIFE: DON'T WASTE IT

Mercia J Tapping

Cover design by SelfPubBookCovers.com
Typesetting by Odyssey Books

THE WINTER OF MY LIFE

Like tattered chards of autumn leaves, I cling to life
Summer is behind me and the impending howl of winter menaces.
The cat meows piteously at his empty bowl
My bowl is empty and it was so full.
I mourn for a life that once was, and will never be again.
I pull my shawl tighter, as if to warm the frozen wasteland within.
The ringing in my ears is my footsteps as I trudge, and trudge some more.
The journey through winter will be long and hard.
But surely, my heart pleads, Spring lies at the end?

Mercia Tapping

TABLE OF CONTENTS

IN MEMORIAM

September 23rd, 2014

It is three years today since my husband Herman died, but in some ways it could have been just yesterday.

Herman was Jewish and we had the service at our local synagogue. It was one of those brilliant clear blue sky days, and I stood outside in the street greeting and hugging my friends and the former employees of my company who had flown in especially to attend the service. No relatives of mine were going to be at the funeral and my husband's family was waiting downstairs in seclusion. We were not on good terms that day. I wanted to be outside in the sunshine.

I waited until everyone in Herman's family was seated and I entered the synagogue alone. I walked with my head held high; I was Herman's wife and proud of it. I walked slowly down the aisle, acknowledging those friends who caught my eye. Later, I was the last person, as was my prerogative, to deliver his eulogy. I needed to find the strength to have my voice heard that day. I had written his eulogy and decided that in my husband's honor, it needed to be the speech of my life and that my love for him should ring out loud and clear and reach every corner of the synagogue. As I got up to speak, I took a few moments to make eye contact with all my friends and employees. I took a deep breath and then my voice rang out clear, strong and unwavering.

This is what I said.

Herman Eulogy

September 23rd, 2011

I have just lost my best friend, my lover and husband, whom over our 16-year relationship gave me the best years of my life. He had a very big heart. Some people never get to have such years or be loved so completely, and for that I am grateful. It was a gift, and I will treasure it forever.

How We Met
Herman used to tell people that he picked me up in a pub in England because no American woman would have him! The truth is we met in 1995 after I advertised in *Boston Magazine* and he replied. We met on Rosh Hashanah and he arrived at my house in the evening, saying he was in disgrace with his sister because he had left the family celebrations early. I thought he was very strange because he peppered me with a thousand screening questions to see whether I would make a suitable life partner. But I always knew from the beginning that we could talk up a storm together, if only I could even begin to understand that Worcester accent of his!

He Made Me Laugh
Above all he made me laugh. He used to think of ways to make me laugh on his way home from work and if he could be outrageous and shock his proper English wife, so much the better. I have countless stories of Herman making me laugh, but know this—sharing laughter with one's spouse is one of the most precious things in life, and we had a lot of laughs together.

We Traveled
We traveled the USA with our timeshares and then we explored Alaska, China and Japan, as well as our best trip of all: an African safari. We

marveled at many of the things we saw and did. Those were very happy times for us and they made for wonderful memories.

We Played Golf, Tennis, Skiied

We were the best of buddies and had great fun together. In the earlier years, we played a lot of tennis and skiied together. In the later years, we were golf partners and he got great pleasure out of seeing me get up the learning curve. In the last two years, there was a role reversal in our golfing partnership. We tried to be the last golfers of the day and I caddied for him, handing him the right club and positioning him to hit in the right direction. I sometimes had a big lump in my throat on these golfing rounds. I would lie about where the ball had landed and kick it into a good spot for him. The guys of Pinehills took over this summer, when he became too much for me to handle. They took him out when he could barely stand upright, but it meant a lot to him. Thank you.

He Loved our Home and Life at Pinehills

It was his dream to come to Pinehills and he twisted my arm to buy our house down here. It turned out to be one of the best things he ever leaned on me to do; it was so good for both of us. He thought Pinehills was like one big day camp and he loved being out and about; whether it was his cribbage, golf or tennis groups, or special Pinehills events. He wanted to take advantage of all the social events and squeeze every piece of fun out of life. He made friends, some wonderful friends who helped us through the last two years of his life. My sister told me this last weekend that pushing me to live at Pinehills was Herman's true legacy to me.

His Last Summer

Over his last two plus months I made a special effort to make sure that the last weeks where he was still ambulatory were ones full of socializing with good friends, and we made final trips to places such as Cape Cod and to the shore, which he truly enjoyed. We even continued, with help from the guys at Pinehills, to get Herman out onto the golf course—even if he had to be half-carried from the golf cart. We tried to make life as normal as possible, even when he was visibly failing. To all our friends who helped make that happen, I cannot thank you enough.

His Courage

I do not think anyone who met Herman over the last couple of years could have failed to have great admiration and deep respect for his courage and his refusal to give into his brain cancer. He was determined to beat the odds and his disease. He never felt sorry for himself and he was determined to carry on as close to normal as possible. In typical Herman fashion he was more concerned about me and how I would fare after he was gone. I think he earned a lot of respect from those around him for his courage, myself included.

I Wish to Thank

I wish to give special thanks to my close friends and the Chix with Stix women in Pinehills for banding together to ease my burdens in the last few weeks of his life. For someone who does not have any blood relatives this side of the Atlantic, I never felt alone or without comfort. I was quite surprised at the outpouring of compassion for me and Herman. But I acknowledge the wisdom of those who orchestrated the help that we got; it was very special and we needed it far more than I could have ever anticipated.

The End

When Herman was lying there in the last few days of his life, unable to eat, drink or swallow, lying there asleep and unresponsive, I was told he could still hear those around him. I believed that it was my last job as his wife to help him transition peacefully from this world to the next. So I would speak to him softly, privately, telling him I was going to be okay after he was gone and it was all right to leave us when he was ready. In the evenings, I crept down in my nightie to kiss him good night, and he astonished me, when I kissed him on the lips, by puckering up and kissing me firmly back. He let me know that he had heard what I was saying to him, what an effort he must have made to kiss me, and I will remember those kisses forever. He was a good man, a brave man and it was a privilege to have been loved by him.

Condolences

So many people are expressing their condolences to me, but I think a better word would be "congratulations". Congratulations for having a love that burned so brightly. Congratulations for living a life together to its fullest, and congratulations for having made the journey with him through his illness to his end.

I will miss him and love him forever.

YOU ARE NEVER COMING BACK: A WIDOW'S WAIL

I had no idea that you were going to change my life
I did not know how to love, until you showed me the way.
You told me every day how much you loved me, and then you were gone.
I held your hand until it was icy cold, incredulous at the slender thread that separates life and death,
And then they took you from me and you were never coming back.
A thousand times I wished to hear your voice just one more time, to feel your gentle touch.
But you were never coming back.
Was that your footsteps I heard at the door?
Perhaps if I just close my eyes and pray, you will return to me,
Alas, that is never going to be.
Instead, I kneel at your grave and my widow's wail rents the air.
The inscription says " Together Forever".
Please tell me why I am supposed to live without you, because I truly do not know.
And you are never coming back.

Mercia Tapping

I thought that after the funeral, my journey through the brutish hell of being a caregiver for a spouse with brain cancer was over, and that I would start anew, and one day a better, life. Little did I know that I was due to be tested again and again. Tested until I envied my husband being in Heaven. I was about to descend into another form of hell.

PROLOGUE: MY VOICE

After Herman died from brain cancer, I went to work and stared aimlessly at my computer screen for months and idled the hours away. I had lost my purpose and passion for life. I had tried so desperately hard over the last two years and five months to give him some joy in his life each day. In the face of the rising beast of Glioblastoma, it had never felt like enough, but at least I knew my purpose on this planet. It was to escort him to the gates of Heaven; my last sacred duty as his wife. And now he was gone. Why was I being left behind?

In earlier days of my life, I knew that I had been a bright light, a source of comfort and inspiration to others; it had been the overriding theme of my entire life. My life had been about educating others about the possibility of having happier and healthy lives. But now the lights were out; I wondered if that vibrant, passionate woman, so excited about her causes was ever going to return.

It was not as if I had solely defined myself by my role as "wife"—far from it, but being married had always given me a safe place, a context in which everything else stood. I had adored my husband, and even becoming successful in the business world was partially fueled by wanting to give him a lifestyle that he had never had, but had always craved. So when I was able to buy a home in Pinehills, MA, overlooking a golf course, my success had helped him fulfil one of his dreams—a summer home.

I had been looking out my living room window at the golf course, but it no longer was a source of pleasure. Rather, it was an unkind reminder that I walked the golf course alone, sometimes with tears streaming down my face, always asking the same question into the wind: "Tell me why I am here. What am I supposed to do with my life? Surely, it is something more than just waiting to die to join him?" But the wind never replied, and I missed the man who used to sit beside me in the golf cart with a big grin on his face. He would say: "We have each other and we have our health, what more do we need?" What more indeed? But I was alone. The lights were out and I had no voice.

To understand what I mean by my voice is to understand that I have been using my gifts of writing and public speaking about the causes I passionately believed in ever since my teenage years. I led a hunger strike for better food at the Catholic boarding school, which I saw as the equivalent of a jail where the inmates were being starved and cruelly abused. I was always tilting at windmills, dreaming of transforming the world in some way. And sometimes I actually managed to transform something. By 2006 my company, AllergyBuyersClub.com, was recognized as the leading woman-owned small business in the USA. We were given countless accolades for its education and products, all of which showed people how they could change their indoor environments in order to better their health. It was a source of great pride to me. I had used my voice to transform the lives of hundreds of thousands of people and felt I had earned my right to breathe the air on this planet.

But during Herman's illness, even my passion for my work evaporated; it no longer seemed important compared to the life and death battle we were fighting together. After all, he was my husband, the man who had told me every day that I had given him the best years of his life, and he was lucky to have found me. This proud, courageous man was losing a piece of his brain every day to this vicious disease for which there was no reprieve, only death. Herman had sometimes accused me of being overly invested in my work, but when the chips are down and your spouse is sick, you make choices. I had made mine. I neglected my business. Of course, I did not think I was neglecting it at the time because, the superwoman that I am thought I could handle it all. Of course, I couldn't. I withdrew from the public eye, stopped speaking and writing. Instead, I worked tirelessly on ways to prolong my husband's life and fight this battle alongside him. Foolish woman that I was, I thought I would bounce back after his death and lead the charge at work once more to dizzying new heights of accomplishment.

Naturally, as the work part of my life resumed, I would be writing again—but about what? The answers were not forthcoming.

I thought about all the newsletters I had written about Herman and myself testing out products at home. One of the most famous posts was our quest for the perfect pillow. Herman loved all our products, and we gaily took apart air purifiers and vacuum cleaners, bounced on mattresses and cleaned everything in sight with our steam cleaners. Since Herman was rather a klutz, I used to joke at work that if a product passed the "Herman Test" then it was consumer friendly enough for any member of the public. Well, Herman was gone, so I would not be writing about our product testing antics again. Then I thought of writing about the so-often ignored plight of the caregiver, a cause which is still near and dear to my heart. I do in fact still support other caregivers via Facebook and in my personal life to this day. But, try as I may, I've never felt moved to write about my caregiver experiences. It was an extraordinarily dark period of my life, and I had no desire to relive it. I just wanted to put it behind me. I thought that perhaps my life as a writer or business leader was sadly over, even though my Brain Cancer Facebook group often told me that my posts were uplifting and inspiring. But I knew better—the woman that I knew and loved was adrift, and she had lost her voice.

I have always had some sense of being able to communicate with the spirit world, but until after Herman's death I had made a conscious decision to stay with my feet firmly grounded on this planet. After his death, as you will learn later in this book, from time to time, he made his existence and presence known in ways with which I could not argue. He wanted me to know, without a shadow of a doubt, that he was my big guardian angel, holding my hand during my journey and pulling some divine strings on my behalf. But messages from beyond sometimes do not make complete sense when you receive them, although in retrospect the messages had crystalline clarity. But I, poor lowly human that I am, stomped around in a fog. I asked Herman endlessly to just tell me what I was supposed to do with my life, so I could get going and return to action. I think, as a CEO, I wanted something like a divine 5-year business plan, all neatly laid out, so I could just set my sights on another goal and make it happen. The answers I got from Heaven were always a puzzle, their meanings so frustratingly outside my comprehension. At some point, I began to accept that I was in a cocoon, and if I was patient, one day the butterfly would fly free again. In the meantime, the voice was still silent.

Of course, it never occurred to me that I would need to endure a major illness to find my voice again. No one in their right mind willingly signs up for that! Part of my journey through breast cancer would be finding my voice and what it is that I am supposed to contribute to the world in this next phase of my life.

During a conversation with a good friend, Pat Henderson, shortly after my diagnosis, I expressed how incredulous and humbled I was by the miracles that were happening in my life, even as I, like my husband before me, faced the dreaded cancer diagnosis. As the news of my diagnosis and the long journey ahead of me became known in my community, I received offers to help me from far and wide. The outpouring of compassion and love for me was quite overwhelming, but as yet I did not fully understand it. As somebody who is by nature quite introverted, abysmally shy in groups of strangers, I had always regarded myself like a rare wine, an acquired taste for those who got to know me well. It was people like Herman who lit up a room whenever he entered, who were the easily lovable ones, but not me. I came to learn just how wrong I was. Pat suggested that I write down the daily miracles in my life, so I could dwell on them instead of the unpleasant aspects of my disease. It then occurred to me that if I did so, that this would be the path through which I would not lose sight of who I am at my core, and indeed rediscover that long lost woman whom I longed to meet again. I reasoned if I wrote a book about my journey and its many miracles and lessons along the way, it could help me heal myself and others who are struggling with any serious disease to find the light, where at first it seems so very dark.

This book chronicles finding my voice and my new purpose for life through and during my breast cancer. Join your hand with mine in this journey, as I will surely travel through the darkest nights of my soul in my quest for healing and light. I hope it will inspire and help you find your own voice. You only have one life, don't waste it.

Lesson learned: A life without a purpose outside of oneself is meaningless. Like flotsam and jetsam I was floating aimlessly around in life. That is no way to live.

BIG ANGELS

Meet some important members of my support team. These people played a very active role in my life, often almost on a weekly basis, and their contribution to my life and to my healing was nothing short of extraordinary. There were legions more supporters and well wishers who gave me car rides, cooked for me, and came to visit than I can possibly name here. But this is an introduction to the main players whom you will see mentioned quite frequently throughout this book.

The Mass General Hospital Team

I cannot say enough good things about this hospital and the team who took care of me. I was always treated with such loving compassion and consideration. They held my hand, listened to my concerns, and imbued in me the confidence to keep going at every step of the way. Each of the three principal members of my team were nothing short of amazing. Dr Kevin Hughes, my surgeon; Dr Aditya Bardia, my oncologist; and Dr Karen Bernstein, my radiation oncologist, along with a legion of nurses and technologists, who accompanied me every step of this journey. To them, I owe my life.

Herman in Heaven

Literally an angel, I always felt my beloved husband was watching over me from Heaven, and his hand showed itself to me unexpectedly when I needed it most. Sometimes he showed up in ways in which it was hard to deny that he truly was around me. Of course, I dearly missed his physical presence and his physical touch, which could have comforted me during my journey. I would have given anything to have him around. I sometimes wept and felt so incredibly alone in making this journey without him. Yet for all that, I always knew he was around me if I needed him; he just existed in another dimension. I learned that I could communicate with him using my psychic abilities, and in the early part of my journey I did so quite often. But I will never deny that I would have preferred that he was still here on Earth helping me with my illness as I had done for him. Making this journey without my spouse was hard. Harder than I would have ever anticipated.

A WIDOW'S LAMENT

Every day you made me laugh
And when you left it made me cry

Dear God, just tell me
Why did he have to die?

Jon Rivers

Jon is probably my biggest angel of all, and is somewhat an enigma. We met through eHarmony in November 2012, when I first put my tremulous foot into the dating pool. He was somewhat ahead of me, having been widowed for longer than I. After countless Skyping sessions and emails, we eventually met in January 2013, and I was totally intrigued and fascinated by him; we spent the weekend together and talked up a storm. Later that same month he alerted me that he suspected financial irregularities in my company, and guided me through discovering the truth.

We agreed shortly after that to remain friends and not to pursue a romantic relationship. I always knew Jon would remain a friend and told him that. How could I not be friends with the man who had alerted me to the financial shenanigans going on in my company? As luck would have it, six weeks later I was contacted by a corporation who had been following my company for years, with the idea of eventual acquisition, and asked if the time was now right. We agreed to proceed to negotiations for them to buy my company. I let Jon know via email that this was happening and thanked him for all his coaching earlier that year. Jon immediately replied and asked if I would like some help with the process, since he had some experience in selling companies. I gratefully accepted his help. We Skyped and emailed pretty regularly for four months, keeping our communication strictly on business matters, tirelessly working together on the acquisition. In early November 2013, suddenly the proposed deal fell through, through no fault of our own. I spontaneously remarked in a Skype session that it was very hard to cram everything I needed to talk to him about into a weekly one-hour Skype session. His response took me aback. He replied that his offer to come and consult to my company, one that he had made earlier this year, was still open.

I knew that I could benefit enormously from his business consulting. I felt there were some divine strings at work, and the next day I accepted Jon's offer. We agreed to meet in Boston in early December 2013. After a two-day visit to my company and seeing for himself all the help we so desperately needed, he suggested that as of January 2014 he would try and come back twice a month, to which I gratefully agreed.

Just before Christmas, after a routine mammogram, I got the news that I needed a biopsy and feared the worst. I told Jon the news and he, amongst others, leaned hard on me to transfer my treatment to Mass General. I could not have made a better decision.

My Facebook GBM Group

Shortly after Herman's death, I joined a private group on Facebook for the present and past caregivers of loved ones with brain cancer. In the year following his death I sponsored the first group in person meet-up for a relaxation and renewal weekend in Plymouth; 16 of us attended the meet-up. My friends opened up their houses to provide accommodation and I cooked up a storm for three days. It was the first of many such future meet-ups around the country. During that weekend I got to know some of these amazing women. I had organized a program of renewal, which included manicures, massages, angel card readings, mediation and tourist sightseeing activities around Plymouth. We ended our weekend with a BBQ hosted by my friends, Noreen and

Peter, and conducted a grand raffle of some of the returns from my warehouse. I got to know and admire some of these women really well. When my own cancer appeared, these same women were available day and night through Facebook, always cheering me on. They made a huge difference to my journey. I could go online to Facebook and never feel alone. In particular, I was alone one night before a chemo infusion and just feeling intensely miserable. Immediately a number of women chimed in and helped me redirect my thoughts to happier times.

Linda Lawlor

Linda took me to the majority of my early chemo infusions. She wasn't someone whom I knew really well before my illness started, but she was definitely a huge miracle to me. She brought such joy and laughter into my life and made hospital visits almost fun. Sometimes I just lay back on my infusion bed and chuckled at her antics! At the time, we recognized that we were both going through a transition in life; hers was a divorce. We talked endlessly about our current life challenges, and envisioned the future that we wanted when we came out the other side. Linda said that she saw me as her guide and mentor through her own transition. Linda's mother died of breast cancer, and I know it pained her to see me go through infusions. But throughout it all, Linda was the personification of lightness and patience, making me laugh, and she showered me with thoughtful, useful little gifts. But most of all, it was her gift of time that was the most valuable to me. Linda did not live locally, and our infusion trips cost her over 200 miles of driving, just in one day alone. That is being a friend.

Sandy Stuart

Sandy runs a bed and breakfast in Plymouth, and I consider her to be my closest girlfriend here. She is a caregiver to her husband who has Alzheimer's and I understand her journey all too well. We continued, throughout my treatment, our ritual of my having dinner together almost once a week, except this time Sandy often cooked for me. In the past, I had done the cooking. She cooked me breakfast treats to take home, and always offered to run errands, even calling me from stores when she was out shopping in case I needed something. She was also a fountain of wisdom on natural remedies to deal with all the side effects of the medicines I was taking. There was nothing she wouldn't do for me if she could. The woman has wings! Sandy is a very religious woman and she believed, as I do, that Jon's appearance in my life was divine intervention. She also is one of the very few friends who knew Herman, and could allow me to reminisce about him and the happier times in my life. Perhaps most importantly, she and I could talk to each other without fear of judgment, and her goodness of heart always shone through. Just being able to text her before I went to bed, to have a little moan about how I hated all my chemo side effects, made a difference.

Rose Weilberg

Rose is a very wise and generous hearted woman in her eighties, who cooked me endless meals, played bridge with me even when I had "chemo brain", and listened to me wail when I needed to. She checked up on me constantly, always concerned for my health. She made a huge difference to me during my journey. Both Rose and I are widows and she understood only too well how lonely it can be to face health challenges without a life partner. I was able to talk to Rose without reserve about my journey, its ups and downs, and my confusion as to where it was all leading. I felt very blessed to have her in my life.

Ann Marcus

Ann is a friend who is a very well-organized problem solver and was infinitely generous with her time. She collected my mail from our post office for months, checked in on me almost daily to see how I was feeling, cooked things like baked apples for me, and always listened, whether I was in the doldrums or feeling far more hopeful. She was a tireless cheerleader. A few months through my journey she and her husband moved to Assisted Living.

While only 25 miles away, it was not the same as being around the corner in the next street, and I missed her. I will always have a special place in my heart for Ann, as her support during Herman's illness was nothing short of extraordinary. I will never forget that.

Debbie Damiano

Debbie appeared out of almost nowhere, although I had known her for years in my book group. Debbie has a background in nursing and she would cheerfully drive me to numerous medical appointments at MGH and sit with me in the doctor's office, asking intelligent additional questions when my anxiety or chemo brain was failing me. She also was prone to appearing at my front door with unexpected gifts of flowers or food that she thought I might like. Her sweetness and generosity of spirit was a source of light in my life, which seemed so dark at times. She never ceased to amaze me throughout my journey. I was blessed to get to know her a great deal better through my journey.

Jan Phillips

Jan was Linda's backup as a driver when she couldn't take me to infusions and would sometimes delight me by turning up with leftovers from one of her catering events. She is very artistic with how she presents food, which was important when my appetite was failing me. Later, when Linda had moved to Florida and my radiation fatigue was being far too insistent, she cheerfully drove me around and kept me company on lonely nights.

Maureen Gendrolius

Maureen is just one of my favorite people. We met through *Chix with Stix*, a ladies golf group, and then became firm friends. She maintained an email list of people who were ready to jump to my aid at a moment's notice. It was so comforting to know that list was so large. Together with another friend, Rosemarie Havens, she organized a birthday party for me a short while after my last chemo infusion, which I will never forget. She also organized a flawless plan for people to drive me to MGH during radiation.

Rosemarie Havens

Rosemarie Havens is a breast cancer survivor and turned to gardening as a career in retirement. She helps maintain my perennials garden. As you will learn later, Rosemarie generously hosted a birthday party for me in June 2014, the best birthday party of my entire life.

Other Supporters

It took a small army of supporters, car drivers and well wishers to get me through my cancer journey, too many to list here. But I appreciate each and every one of them. Each conversation, card, gift or car ride was precious. I could never have made it alone.

Lesson learned: People cannot help you until you tell them what is going on with your life. Then prepare to be delightfully surprised with the goodness of humanity. I was surprised over and over again.

AND SO IT BEGAN

January 15th, 2014

I arrived at Mass General Hospital, accompanied by my friend Sandy, for a biopsy. I knew from the look on the radiologist's face last month at my local hospital that this was not going to be routine. The messages I had gotten from my beloved Herman in Heaven, before I even had the first mammogram in December, alerted me that I was in trouble. But I had no idea what lay before me that day at MGH. Upon admission, Dr Kevin Hughes, the co-head of the breast cancer unit, informed me before the biopsy even took place that I was going to be a chemotherapy patient. What? You have to be kidding me! I had just had two routine manual breast examinations by local doctors within the last three months and now I was being told that one of my tumors was several centimeters long! In other words, it was not a small lump, and it should have been detected earlier. That day was a dizzying whirlwind of 3D mammograms, ultrasounds, biopsies (yes, there were multiple tumors) and a breast MRI. The team at MGH wasted no time, and appointments for me were magically and instantly procured. Mine was a case that clearly should not be delayed. I heard that I was going to have five months of chemotherapy in order to shrink the tumors before surgery. I told Dr Hughes that if breast conservation was possible, I would prefer that. He said no promises, but he would try his best. I was in shock. I had always dreaded breast cancer ever since my mother had a mastectomy some 30 years earlier. And now what I had dreaded most was upon me. I was offered a visit with a social worker and I accepted. While I'm normally a courageous woman, at that moment I could only shake in fear. Tears rolled down my face in small rivers. "Why me?" I asked. Haven't I suffered enough in recent years? My husband had died of brain cancer, my life savings had been decimated after propping up the company. And now this? Images of nausea, hair loss, and breast mutilation presented themselves in rapid succession. I clung to Sandy's hand. How much was any person supposed to bear?

GOING PUBLIC WITH BREAST CANCER
January 17th, 2014

Adapted from a post on Facebook:

My friends,

It is now time to go public and tell you all that I have stage 3B breast cancer. I am being treated at Mass General Hospital by some of the best doctors in the world. I have great faith in them and also in their superior diagnostic equipment, which has detected cancer beyond the breast onto the chest wall and lymph nodes. The exact amount of the spread has not yet been determined. My entire 2014 will be spent fighting for my life, with a sequence of chemotherapy, surgery, and then radiation. I have about 2-3 weeks to get my affairs in order, which range from doing my taxes and assembling my home wellness support team, to getting fitted for wigs, as I will lose 100% of my lovely hair. Whether I lose an entire breast and have a mastectomy depends on how well, amongst other things, I respond to chemotherapy. A good friend is backing me up to help me run my business during my treatment journey, when I anticipate that I will have to take a great deal of time off work. Naturally, this has been a devastating blow, occurring just as I thought I was starting to rally, after losing my husband to brain cancer and finally sorting out my company from the internal financial mismanagement that had occurred while he was sick. So this warrior woman is wearily picking up the sword again. Of course I will fight, it is in my DNA. I can never lose hope that one day I will regain my health, that my business will prosper, and a man who loves me will be at my side again. I have learned, or am attempting to learn, several things that I will share with you all. Firstly, you have to consciously choose life if you are to fight for it, and have faith that there is a purpose for that life, which is as yet unrevealed. Secondly, there is no point in asking "why me?" The sooner that I learn to accept the reality of what is before me, the sooner the healing will begin. If I argue with reality, then reality always wins. Thirdly, even in this sea of desolation, there are miracles in my life on a daily basis if I choose to see them—and I am making that choice. Already, the people who know of my illness are showing me an incredible amount of love and that is humbling and I feel blessed. I know this is not a journey I can make alone, and at many times it will seem like a very dark night of the soul. I tell you all now that the caterpillar may be in its winter cocoon, but one day she will joyously fly free again. God bless you and go in good health.

Lesson learned: Why me? Why not me? I knew intellectually that peace comes with acceptance of what is. But this journey was going to turn out to be more challenging than I ever imagined. The struggle for my mind to rise above it all was the fiercest battle of all.

LET'S CONCENTRATE ON MIRACLES, NOT GRIEF
January 25th, 2014

Let's concentrate on the miracles and good news in my life. I have been finally cleared of cancer spreading to other major organs, and therefore, I am told, I have a 90% chance of a cure. I am still working against the clock to get all parts of my life handled before I start phase one, the five months of chemotherapy, commencing on February 4th. Treatment of various kinds will continue all year. But I am filled with love from all those who are volunteering to help me, and it is in that abundance of love that I realize that my grief as a widow has now gone. I will always love Herman, but the grief, for the moment at any rate, has all but evaporated.

January 21st was Herman's birthday. I would normally have gone to the cemetery, but that day I was in Mass General getting my marching orders for treatment from my oncologist, Dr Bardia. I lifted my eyes up to Heaven and said: "Happy birthday, Honey. Sorry, but I have other priorities right now." I realized in that moment that I had reached another phase in my grieving process. I could not grieve and fight for my life at the same time. I will never stop missing the man who loved me so well and unconditionally. We had a beautiful life together, and those days were blessed indeed, but now my focus is on restoring my health, which I know is what Herman would have wanted me to do.

Lesson learned: Start looking for daily miracles even in the darkest of days. If you look for them, you will find them. These miracles will make you smile, as they will remind you of the goodness in humanity, often when you least expect it.

FIRST ROUND OF CHEMO STARTING SOON
February 2nd, 2014

On Tuesday, February 4th, 2014, I will start the first phase of my healing journey with the first of eight rounds of chemotherapy, over a period of 20 weeks. With surgery and radiation to follow, this treatment process is going to take up my entire year. That year seems to stretch out in front of me like infinity. But I am not going to let cancer define me as a person or let me wallow in my misery, although I know I will have crappy days. Rather, I will be the person that I have always been, doing what I always do, and by the way, I temporarily have cancer that needs treatment. I have a deep and unwavering conviction that I will beat cancer and am designing a self-guided meditation where the army of the light overcomes the army of the dark. If I could walk on hot coals in my youth, I can surely harness the power of the mind to kill cancer cells.

Lesson learned: You have to consciously choose to live. It is a choice. I made the choice to fight and live, and trust that I would find out why saving my life was important. Many were the times people have told me that they do not know if they would have the courage to go through what turned out to be a very vigorous year of treatment. But first of all, you have to find the will to live.

FIRST ROUND OF CHEMO OVER
February 5th, 2014

Yesterday, February 4th, was a 13-hour day at MGH, which included an operation for the insertion of a smart port (love that morphine!) for all future blood draws and infusions; the requisite monitoring of vital signs, a visit with my oncologist, who patiently answered my next list of questions (I will always have many!) and six hours of infusions which included one chemo agent and two antibodies. Throughout my day at MGH I was treated with loving care, and lots of attention from a nurse, Barbara, in my infusion private room, who will be with me through the next 18 months. On subsequent visits, in addition to the constant food and snacks offered, I can have free Reiki, acupressure and massage, all in 15-minute sessions, while I recline in my bed like a princess. Ably assisted, of course, by my friend Linda, whose bubbly, loving energy added to the day's fun. The Decadron (steroid) I was taking had me wired and I talked for about 15 hours non stop. Oh my!

The good news is that during the next three months of infusions (four times over twelve weeks), it looks as if I will be tolerating side effects pretty well and will be able to maintain a normal life without too much interruption. I am not experiencing nausea today, the day after my first infusion. Following these first four chemotherapy rounds, I get another four infusions over eight weeks, consisting of two heavy-duty chemo agents only. This is when it is predicted that my hair will finally fall out and I will be combatting a lot of nausea and loss of appetite as well as increasing fatigue. It is also when I anticipate that I will start to need more support. I told my oncologist that I had a few extra pounds to contribute to this good cause, so I hope he did not mind if I lost some! He was cool about this.

After a 4 to 6-week gap following chemotherapy, I will have some kind of operation, the severity of which depends on how I have reacted to the chemotherapy program and reduced my tumors (I have multiple, and spread outside the left breast but no major organ spread). After another approximately 6-week gap, I will have about 6-7 weeks of daily radiation. During post surgery and radiation I anticipate that I will be reaching out for help to my friends. Of course, I had thought that at the end of 2014 that my treatment would be finished. My infusion nurse broke the bad/good news to me that next year (2015) I will have infusions of antibodies every three weeks until May. However, she said that this will not give me much in the way of side effects or hair loss. I will be prescribed these antibodies because my tumors are "triple positive" and my team are very confident of a long-term cure.

I have decided that, throughout this, I will do everything I can to not lose sight of who I am as a person. My primary identity will not be that of a breast cancer patient, and I intend to continue to contribute to the health and wellbeing of others. I can truly tell you all that it does not occur to me for one moment that I will not beat this (so please do not keep telling me that I will!). I am who I am, and for the moment at any rate, I also have cancer in the background.

I always wondered after Herman's death how I would find my voice and write again. Never did I dream it would be through this! So what I will be writing about is the everyday miracles that I encounter along the way, which, if you pay attention, are available to everyone. My writing will eventually become a book designed to inspire others. I feel very strongly that I will discover that love is my guide, love is my protection, and love is my reward at the end of this journey. I am already profoundly moved by all the extraordinary love and caring that has already been shown to me by so many. It has filled the inner emptiness and loneliness that I have felt as a widow and I feel blessed.

Lesson learned: Even in the midst of darkness you can find laughter and light. Who would have thought it possible to laugh on the first day of chemotherapy? Who would ever guess that this was going to be a period in my life where I felt more love than any other period in my life?

REALITY
February 8th, 2014

Not so fast! There is an annoying reality to getting chemotherapy; it slows even me down! My life is now in slow motion. I creep around, with great effort, from one end of the room to the other like a darn turtle, and have great difficulty swallowing. But on the bright side, except for fatigue, the other side effects are starting to lift. The idea of pacing myself will be a novel, although temporary, way of life. Naturally, my Siamese cats are happy to keep me company at night, but I am having to train Truffles that leaping on and off the bed via landing on my chest, where the port wound is still raw, is simply not appreciated!

This is also when I can pat myself on the back for my manic "getting ready" preparations of the last few weeks. I must have enough supplies to equip a survivalist underground shelter, and a few of my favorite soups are already happily freezing. I think, unfortunately, that this cook might be taking a bit of a vacation. However, miracles are still in abundance. The local market at Pinehills has told me that as long as I give them 48 hours notice, they will cook any of my favorite takeout foods, sell the majority to the general public and reserve whatever I want for my own consumption! Even deliver to me if need be. How good is that!?

Perhaps the biggest miracle of all this week is that my first wig arrived, and it is really like my own hair. It is bad enough being a chemotherapy patient, but I do not want to look like one! So I am as prepared as anybody can be for the eventual reality of losing my hair, all the while knowing that the day I have to shave my head will be profoundly sad. Quite frankly, it is one of the things I dread most. But I have been told repeatedly that after chemotherapy, hair can grow back curly—now that would be a treat! All my life I have wanted natural curls. In the meantime, looking on the bright side, I will be saving on my usual hairdresser bills and indulging in some decadent aromatherapy massage instead. And if even I don't sparkle as much, my nails will continue to have double sparkles!

WORKING AND PROUD OF IT
February 10th, 2014

Very proud of myself. Drove to work and made it through six hours at the office. Of course, I was totally wasted tonight. I have discovered this new miracle "eat as much as you want" weight loss diet. Guaranteed to have the pounds drop off you! There is just one hitch, it is called chemotherapy and you get mouth sores and have difficulty swallowing. My tastebuds have gone completely haywire already, even in week one. Everything tastes bitter, carbonated beverages sting the roof of my mouth. Food is very hard to chew. I swear I will be on the adult version of baby food by the end of this and I will have forgotten that teeth were meant for chewing. Chemotherapy is not for sissies!

ONE WEEK POST CHEMO
February 12th, 2014

One week post chemo, and pretty much as the oncologist predicted, I am feeling close to normal. I actually enjoyed my dinner last night. Of course, my new mission as a cook is to figure out "1001 Recipes for Ground Beef (or chicken, turkey, etc.) to tempt a chemo patient". I have to eat very slowly and chew, chew, chew! I now have two blissful weeks till the next wave. I am off to work this morning and back in fearless leader mode.

I CAN CHEW AGAIN
February 16th, 2014

Never was I so grateful today to find myself being able to chew again, so maybe I won't be confined to baby food after all! But my tastebuds have already changed radically. A few brave souls have invited me over for dinner. Sometimes, they hit it just right and I am just thrilled and grinning from ear to ear that something actually tastes good, while other poor hosts have been subjected to me grimacing after the first bite, while another "absolutely can't stand it" food gets added to the list. It is anything tart and acidic that sets me off, but my favorite home-made granola bites are like razor blades in my mouth, and I can forget fizzy drinks. As for wine, it tastes pretty disgusting. Bread tastes like cardboard. The no-no list keeps growing. Meanwhile, my collection of gourmet balsamic vinegars is going to age gracefully.

Of course, I have been trying to catch up at work like crazy, but I need to pace myself better. I achieved a first in my business career by needing to crash on my office couch for two hours last Friday, complete with the shivers. I have also been fighting a cold (where the heck did that come from?). So whenever I get a nice spurt of energy I get as much work done as possible. This coming week will be the best in this cycle and so I intend to enjoy the "new normal" before the next chemotherapy round on February 25th. I think I am like one of those little people in the cuckoo clock—now you see me, now you don't.

A MIRACLE AT WORK
February 19th, 2014

An amazing thing happened to me today. I was called into a meeting and, to my surprise, all my staff were there. OMG, I thought, what crisis has hit us today, since we have had more than our fair share? To my surprise, I was handed a pink rubber bracelet that said, "Cele-brate Courage," and then all my staff solemnly put on pink bracelets, which I was told that they are committed to wearing until the day I am declared cancer free, at which time we will have a bracelet cutting ceremony. I was quite overcome, as you can imagine!

On another note, my hair is falling out at a rapid pace, but I am more at peace with losing it. Or to be more truthful, resigned to the inevitable.

I followed the advice to test-drive a wig before that dreaded "go bald" day. So I have been doing just that for a couple of days. Every time I put it on, I can smile at the reflection in the mirror and say, "Well hello, there is that lovely woman again." And when my eyelashes fall out, trust me, I will be batting false ones! So tonight off I truck to CVS to get one of my endless prescriptions. Thank goodness for Medicare. Then the pharmacist exclaimed, "Mercia, your hair looks simply lovely!" So I fessed up as to why, and urged her to send people up to MGH when she can. They are a wonderful hospital staff. She is adding me to her prayer list and we talked for the longest time.

I think I will be meeting just the most lovely humans on this journey.

And now that I can chew again… forget weight loss. I have been making up for lost time!

SECOND CHEMO DOWN
February 26th, 2014

I am surviving the second chemotherapy round quite well. My biggest issue is insomnia from the steroid, and with only four hours sleep for last two nights, I look haggard. However, the last steroid dose is tonight, so I should start to slowly pick up and regain a normal sleep pattern.

Other side effects, with some rigid diligence, are being controlled and the blood work so far is good, although there are a couple of serious watch points.

I made the nurse dizzy with my steroid motor mouth as I peppered her for almost an hour with well researched questions about managing side effects and alternative options; she could not argue with my sources for the questions. She was a bit desperate with the time overrun. There was no arguing with the intelligence of my questions, and she needed some MD specialist input to give me answers.

Of course, when I told her that I intended to disappear my tumors by the time my chemotherapy was over, and that I believed in mind over matter since I had walked on hot coals 30 years ago, she began to see that I was not the normal kind of patient. So she referred me to their mind-body specialist at MGH, a well known psychologist, Ann Webster. The nurse said pointedly, "You two would be a good match"—sub silent text—"you are both crazy!"

My lovely hair is now a thing of the past, sadly cut ultra short to fit neatly under wigs. Cutting my hair short was exceptionally emotionally painful. I knew it had to be done, because my hair was coming out in clumps, but it was a gut-wrenching experience. At least, I comforted myself, my first wig makes me feel normal and actually look quite lovely again. I am now ordering and will be trying out different wigs and also have started using a gel that is supposed to preserve my eyebrows and lashes through chemotherapy. A girl has to do what a girl has to do, since it is clear that I will be wearing wigs for a long time. I am working with a hair expert in CA over feeding my hair bulbs even while in chemotherapy, so that when it grows back it will be healthy and strong.

So I am fighting for my recovery and being my own patient advocate. After all, what else would you all expect from me? I am no wuss, although I admit to being human and having my wobbly, teary moments. I never will say any of this is easy. It is not.

Lesson learned: It is not how you fall down but how you get up that counts. I fear I will be doing a lot of falling down in the next few months. I have a premonition that this journey is going to get a whole lot worse before it gets better.

A HAPPY DAY
March 8th, 2014

Last night, after I awoke from three hours of sleep, I said, "What the heck, I am fed up with insomnia," and took 1/2 mg of Ativan and then slept the sleep of the just. The insomnia is related to steroid use and it really gets to me at times. However, I was able today to be awake enough for my brain to kick into gear so I could discuss work issues with Jon during the morning. He was pleased with our progress. The weather in Plymouth had reached a balmy 50 degrees, so we drove down to Plymouth harbor and walked around for an hour in the sunshine; both the sky and water were the purest of blues. It felt so good to be outdoors after over two months of being indoors only. I was happy just walking alongside a man, a dear friend whom I have come to deeply care for and respect. When we came back I was exhausted and it was nap time for two and a half hours. Jon comes back in eight days, Monday, March 17th, which is the day before my next chemotherapy round, and as such will be my best day of the month. Then we are going to see how it works out for me to stay at home, with him caring for me in the evenings, while he runs my business during the day. On the other hand, my bed and breakfast girlfriend Sandy has looked after me so well in the first two rounds of abysmal post-chemo 48 hours, but I don't like to impose. Jon and I have agreed that his staying at my house on my lower level is an experiment.

MIND AND BODY
March 12th, 2014

I spent a productive day at Mass General. I had a medication consult with a psychiatrist about my medication-induced insomnia. After an hour of answering a thousand "no's" while she did her due diligence about any history with depression, drugs, etcetera and coming up empty handed, she finally realized my lack of sleep was really simply just steroid-induced insomnia. When she wanted to put down a diagnosis of "adjustment disorder", I suggested she just put down a diagnosis of "insomnia" and I said firmly that there was no adjustment disorder. She is looking at new meds for me. She said I was doing remarkably well, especially as I told her that my next appointment that same day was at the Mind-Body center, because I wanted to discuss how I was going to disappear the cancer cells by the end of chemotherapy.

So off to the Mind-Body center. Now we are talking my kind of talk and playing my kind of game. The head of the center, Ann Webster, a psychologist, walks in to the room. She looks about my age and is a redhead. She looks at me with my kick-ass red wig and says, "How do you like being a redhead?" I grinned and said, "I love it! Of course, there's not much of the real stuff left anymore."

Thankfully, despite the lengthy intake form, which she did not torture me with, she quickly realized that I was in fine mental shape. One of the final questions on the form was "Name three things you want to change about yourself." My only answers were that I wanted to lose a few pounds, kick my cancer cells into oblivion and get my hair back. To be honest, I like myself. I did all the personal growth work that one could ever need some 30 years ago, and I told Ann that my life wasn't about myself but about giving back to the world. She understood. She said I had a wonderful spirit and loved that I was writing about miracles during my journey and that she completely understood the psychic dimensions and happenings in my life. If I can walk on hot coals in my youth, surely I can harness my mind to disappear cancer cells? That is the game I am playing, and finally I have found someone who does not think I am crazy at all but will partner with me. I will see her again soon.

Lesson learned: At the time, I was rather affronted by the questions and the probing by the psychiatrist. Later, as the months progressed and the struggle for my psyche grew more intense, I understood why she needed to ask what she did.

CHEMO INFUSION #3
March 18th, 2014

Infusion #3 out of 8. All news from my blood work report was good. My tumors have shrunk significantly already, and I am clearly responding to treatment. My liver is trending in the right direction; glucose is stable (so my cutting down on sugar clearly helps), neuropathy stable, white and red cell blood counts good. I also lost two pounds, but as I told my oncologist, Dr Bardia, this weight was exactly what I weighed on January 1st, before this mess began. He congratulated me and said that was no mean achievement as the Decadron (steroid) blows people up with bloating. I have seen reports on the Internet of weight gain of up to 60 pounds in breast cancer patients. I must not allow that to happen; I have fought too hard for my weight loss post-Herman's death. My surgery will most probably be early August, and could be a bit earlier or later. The team at MGH will move as fast as my blood count allows, bearing in mind that the second set of chemotherapy treatments will be more onerous.

COURAGE

Courage is not noisy or flamboyant.
It does not shout to the world "Look at me!"
Rather, courage is taking one more step,
When there are no more steps to take
And then one more, again and again.

Mercia Tapping

THIS WEEK
March 19th, 2014

Jon came to Boston on Monday afternoon, the day before my chemotherapy infusion, and we worked hard at the business together. I feel much calmer with his firm management at the helm. I was very anxious last week, and we still have a challenging mountain to climb together, but he is clearly stepping up his involvement with my company.

I am glad to be in my own home and not at Sandy's B&B after my chemotherapy, as packing and getting ready for a trip was getting to be onerous, as I have to remember to take with me every conceivable over-the-counter remedy for side effects and prescribed meds. On top of that, although Ron, her husband and fellow Brit, loves me, he is very possessive of Sandy's time and complains of feeling neglected, so I did not want to overstay my welcome.

CANCER AND STRESS
March 23rd, 2014

The six years preceding my cancer diagnosis were exceptionally stressful and, despite being the strong resilient woman that I am, I nevertheless wondered periodically if my health would finally break under the pressure. To give you some idea of the life stresses I faced, so incredibly close to one another, I will roll the clock back over the last decade. Was I an accident waiting to happen? I will never know, but it has given me pause for deep thought as I ponder about the lifestyle I want to create next after my cancer has been cured. It surely needs to be less stressful.

2003: My mother died.

2007: My cat Fudge died, and a few weeks later my father died. I held his hand for 48 hours till he passed.

2008-2009: Endured very painful sciatica; looked for a new office; cleared, staged and got a house ready for sale—all by myself.

2009: May 14th, Moved into summer home in Plymouth.

2009: June 2nd, Herman, my husband, diagnosed with stage 4 incurable brain tumor, Glioblastoma.

2009-2011: Caregiving years.

2011: Sept 23rd, Herman died.

2012: Grieving. Tried to sell business.

2013: Internal financial mismanagement discovered, tried to sell business.

2014: Jan, Breast cancer diagnosis and treatment during 2014.

I had not been neglecting my health after Herman's death. Far from it, I was on a mission to create a new and very healthy lifestyle. I had taken cooking light classes for over a year to get some new ideas and tastes, as well as to discover what I liked to eat. I had discovered that this was clearly very different from the food I had prepared to cater to my husband's more conservative tastes. This cooking odyssey was a real source of pleasure for me. I also signed up for a weight loss class, and over two years had lost 45 pounds. I wasn't at my goal weight, but I was well on my way. I had scheduled every conceivable routine check up, including a mammography, which had come back negative in 2012.

I had regular deep massages to help ensure my sciatica never returned, and I worked hard at a pilates studio to improve my core strength and fitness. At the same time, I was working on an outer makeover. I bought new clothes to fit my shrinking body and had other clothes altered, while giving a great deal of my ugly "fat" wardrobe away. I was experimenting with new makeup, new hair styles. In other words, I was intent on rediscovering the beautiful and vibrant woman who had been crushed during the caregiving years.

By early 2013, I was actually proud of my progress, and others remarked at how well I had been doing. I had taken up bridge again, a passion from earlier years and put to one side during my marriage, and I had dusted off my golf clubs with the idea of improving my game and taking a few lessons. The social butterfly had been learning to spread her wings again, whether being sociable with friends or sticking a tremulous foot into the dating pool and finding that I was still very much alive as a woman. I was inviting friends over to dinner, getting on planes to see others all over the country. I joined book groups, and delighted in pottering around in my garden. I was beginning to feel truly alive again. I found myself laughing and appreciating life and living. I did not yet know the clear direction for the next phase of my life, but I was optimistic. So much so, I found that once again I had emotional room to take care of others whom I loved in my life. Many friends were the recipients of samples of my cooking adventures, which were delivered to their homes when they were sick, or just to bring a smile to their faces.

I share all this with you because I was just beginning to think, after all the years of suffering and having to rise up to face adversity, that the tide was beginning to turn in my favor. My business, or so I thought, was profitable, my health check ups had all been good, and I had even met a man, Jon, a fellow widower, whom my instincts told me was a man worth getting to know a whole lot better. The winds seemed to be set fair. Then my life quickly unraveled in terrifying and unpredictable ways. I never saw it coming.

Lesson learned: Enjoy the present as you never know when it may change in an instant. This was one of the most important and difficult learnings of my journey, which I needed to learn over and over again. It is probably one of the most difficult lessons for us all.

HAIR, A WOMAN'S CROWNING GLORY
March 24th, 2014

I have had a love affair with my hair ever since I left high school, and when I went to college, I promptly grew it to shoulder length with bangs; longer hair was something my mother had always forbade me to have as a child. So, as you might predict, after leaving school, I promptly threw off the strictures of the ugly short back and sides foisted on me by my well meaning but controlling mother. The one thing I have always kept with any hairstyle as an adult has been my bangs, but other than that, my hair has been a sandbox for flamboyant experimentation my entire life.

I was blessed with an exceptionally thick head of hair. Hairdressers always commented on its thickness; some had the audacity to charge me extra for drying it! While naturally brunette with auburn high-lights, I have colored my hair from auburn, brunette and eventually to various shades of blonde, often highlighted. It did not take me too long as an adult to disavow straight hair and, trust me, it was NEVER short. That mandatory hairstyle of my childhood, which resembled the result of a saucepan over ones head and cut around it, was never going to see the light of day as an adult.

So the first thing anyone noticed about me, apart from a slender figure and ample breasts in my youth, was the lady had HAIR! Ever since I was 30 years old, I had gone to the hairdresser every week; it was one of my guilty pleasures. I walked out of that hair salon every

Friday night, ready to be admired afterwards by the male gender, and most importantly, my husband. Every time I came back from the hairdresser, Herman demanded to look at me and to turn around so he could admire. Often, he would accompany me to the salon, and sit and kibbutz with all the ladies. He would make them laugh, and then grandly announce he was paying my bill, after involving the whole hair salon as to where he should take his beautiful wife for dinner. When he became sick, we still had the same routine, but the staff used to help him out of the car so he could still watch the ladies have their hair done. As he got sicker, he just slept in the car, waiting for me to finish. But he still admired my blonde curly hair, even when he was dying in his hospice bed.

After his death, I realized in my quest and rediscovery of myself that I no longer wished to be blonde, but wanted to return to the more auburn tints of my youth. It was part of finding myself again after grieving and reinventing myself as a gorgeous older woman, and I was intent on a makeover from head to toe. Weight, clothing, nails, makeup and my hair were all getting attention. And a hairstyle change was on the list; no time to look frumpy. I was on a roll.

So imagine my horror some ten months before my cancer diagnosis, when I noticed thinning hair on my crown, which turned into a huge bald patch. Many theories were floated around at the time as to the reason; over processed hair, low thyroid, a stress breaking point—all the while my hair was growing but then breaking off again very rapidly, despite the hair growth supplements I was chowing down. Certainly, the onset could be traced back to the discovery of the "financial irregularities" in my company—perhaps that was the straw that broke the camel's back? Since then, I had been surviving elevated stress levels for several years quite well, or so I thought. I decided to have an analysis of my hair bulbs done before I started chemotherapy, to find exactly the cause of my hair problems. The hair analysis showed malnourished hair bulbs, and I was an accident waiting to happen.

Therefore, when I started chemotherapy, I knew that I wasn't going to be able to hang onto my hair for very long. I always had a horror of looking at bald headed women with scarves walking the halls of Dana Farber hospital during my husband's cancer. I know that many women show their bald heads as a badge of courage. I genuinely applaud them, but I made a different decision. I decided I wanted to look as normal as possible and wear a wig so as not have people staring at me, thinking, "Oh that poor chemo patient." I thought if I wore a wig, people would see me as normal, and then I would rise to the occasion and feel and behave closer to normal. I was not looking for sympathy; although, trust me, later I grew to lean heavily on my support network.

I went looking for wigs; there are some marvelous ones around, but very few in a large cap size. I was initially in a panic as to whether I could locate a suitable one in the right size and color. This was a very important quest, as I realized quickly that I would be wearing a wig outside the house for probably two years (remember short, straight, pixie haircuts are not for me!). Luckily, with the help of a knowledgeable hairdresser, I located my first kick-ass auburn-colored wig.

Then came the fateful day when I went to my usual weekly hairdressing appointment and, after half my hair was left in the sink after washing, my hairdresser Kim finally said it was time. We drew the shades and three people gathered around in the empty salon, all with tears trickling down their faces and one holding my hand. I just sobbed as the last of my lovely hair got cut (not shaved) to about an inch long. I gasped at the sight of myself in the mirror; there, staring at me, was an elderly, almost bald woman. Trust me, you may learn to accept it, but it is not a pretty sight. I was totally repulsed by my appearance—what a sad sight! Then we placed the new wig on my head and I reluctantly realized that this was going to be the beginning of my new face to the world, and for a very long time.

I learned slowly to accept my new bald-headed reflection in the mirror, but I can say truthfully that it never ever gave me any pleasure or pride that I was a courageous breast cancer patient. Rather, it was a wake-up call each morning, and a rude reality check that, with the aid of chemotherapy, I was in a life and death struggle. I may not have made my illness the entire focus of my life, but nor could I ignore it.

My balding head was proof. So each morning I got up, tried to find a flattering outfit in my wardrobe, even on an "at home day," put on my makeup and, if I was going out, I donned one of my wigs. Putting on my wig was a ritual that actually gave me pleasure, as I could breathe a sigh of relief that the beautiful woman was not entirely lost to me. I could smile at her in the mirror and breathe and say, "The beautiful woman is back—there she is again. She is not lost forever." And that feeling was an extraordinary relief.

One of the most surprising and miraculous results of wearing a wig was the enormous number of people who quite spontaneously and genuinely told me how terrific and well I looked. And some told me that they loved my hair and that I looked gorgeous! This genuinely buoyed my spirits, because the energy that I absorbed from them was uplifting and joyful, and not mournful, "oh poor you" sympathy. And in my mind over matter commitment, I wanted to feel better and not wallow in maudlin self pity of "why me?"

For those of you who want to know information about wigs, I was advised to get a synthetic wig because it would be lighter, and one that had a monofilament construction. That advice turned out to be very helpful. Even the lightest of wigs do add extra weight to your head. Luckily for me, my chemotherapy was in winter and spring, so I didn't have a sweating scalp in the dog days of summer. However, I did buy some baby washcloths just in case I hit some heat waves in June 2014, my last month of chemotherapy. I was told my own hair would start growing in August 2014. In the meantime, I was told I would have hair loss everywhere—eyebrows, lashes, facial and body hair. At least, I consoled myself, my hairdressing and eyebrow waxing bills would be down for a long while. Meanwhile, I greedily absorbed all those compliments of "Darling, you look fabulous!"

Lesson learned: In fact, my hair grew back exceptionally slowly, at about 1/4 inch a month, so wigs clearly were a very important part of my wardrobe for a very long time.

HAIR

When I lost my hair, my heart was broken,
The chemo dragon had surely spoken.
With one lick of its beastly flame,
I wondered if I could ever be the same.
With a poison laden dart of tongue
My youth from me was surely wrung.
The old woman in the mirror stared at me,
Who on earth, I asked, was she?
A wig was gently placed onto my head,
It made me smile with fiery red!
That lovely woman is so far from lost,
But breast cancer exacts its painful cost.
My real hair will grow again for sure
And I will both thrive again and endure.

Mercia Tapping

THE ACE OF HEARTS
March 24th, 2014

On Sunday, some very tolerant friends came to play bridge over at my house despite the chemo affecting my memory and concentration. We were on the fourth hand, and it was my turn to deal the first round. For some strange reason when I had finished dealing we were one card short. Frustrated, I re-dealt twice and we all stood up and shook our clothes and looked under the table. But annoyingly, whichever way we looked or re-dealt the cards, there were only 51 cards in the deck, despite the pack having only being used 15 minutes ago. At this point, one of my companions sensibly suggested we could get by with using only one deck of cards. I reluctantly took the offending pack of cards over to the kitchen, grumbling that things just don't disappear off the planet. As I went to put the deck of cards into its sleeve, I noticed a single card laying face down in the sleeve. Then I announced the strange but miraculous discovery of the missing card to my companions. One of them, psychically gifted like myself, said, "Mercia, you know what card it is don't you?" I replied, "Yes, I do, the Ace of Hearts." I took the card out of the sleeve, turned it over, and indeed it was the Ace of Hearts. My friend continued, "And you do know what that means?" I stood with tears streaming down my face. Yes, I did know. "Herman is with us tonight and he wants me and all of you to know that love is my protection, love is my guide and love will be my reward for my journey with cancer." We were all stunned into silence, trying to digest what had just happened.

I had come to realize very early on after my husband passed away that his presence was still very much around me, guiding me, loving me and intervening to send me the help that I needed.

But sometimes I wondered whether I was just imagining his voice and guidance. This was an event that could not be explained away. After that night, I imagined myself having the Ace of Hearts as a breast shield as I went into battle with long flowing red hair, riding on a white horse. That image and memories of that night stayed with me a long time.

Lesson learned: There truly is another heavenly existence, and my husband was with me all the way, loving me throughout this journey. This realization was immensely profound and I needed to remind myself of this countless times, since it gave me great comfort.

MIRACLES ABOUND
March 25th, 2014

Since I have told you that this book includes the miracles that I am experiencing during my journey through breast cancer, I thought it only appropriate to pause to discuss what I mean by the term.

To me, a miracle is something large or small, the perfect answer to your prayers, which arrives when you least expect it, but when you need it most. Call them everyday miracles if you will, although the miracles that have already happened in my life would be deemed far from ordinary or mundane. I often marvel at the hand of God that is so clearly still at work during my suffering. Some people whom I refer to as "Big Angels" have already appeared, rescuing me and sometimes appearing from the most unexpected places. Their generosity of spirit always moves me to tears. But there are the little miraculous events that happen on a daily basis, which simply appear just when I need them, and they smooth my path.

To receive miracles you need to be ready to receive them. First of all, you need to slow down enough to pay attention to what is happening around you. Miracles are there for everyone to pick up, like shiny pennies to put in your pocket.

Of course, I am being forced to slow down during my illness, and the music that fills my house now is slower meditative music, instead of boogying around the house to Zumba. It only took 48 hours after my first chemotherapy treatment to realize that I had come to a skidding halt, but the stillness brought with it a gift of time for inner reflection and space to appreciate the miracles that had been happening in my life.

Being conscious of the everyday miracles is a deliberate choice. You have to choose to both see and receive them. I have been constantly amazed at the little miraculous gestures that people have done or offered to ease my day. Examples include the local food market, who offered a personal delivery service if I was unable to pick up pre-cooked food, or the car inspection service who inspected my car without my having the requisite paperwork all in hand, or the pharmacy jumping me in the queue to fill a new prescription, knowing that I was returning home after an infusion day. It has been a myriad of little things that happened on a daily basis to reduce my stress levels when every little chore loomed like a mountain. These miracles made me smile, laugh, and gave me joy when I least expected it. I received thoughtful cards, flowers to brighten my day, or a last-minute invitation to a quiet dinner from an understanding friend such as Rose, who could appreciate that I wanted to be sociable but was not at my effervescent best. An enthusiastic complement on my wig, and how well I was looking, made me smile. None of these things were expected, but they were little joys and made life so much sweeter.

Of course, there have already been very big miracles along the way and the "angels" such as Jon, who stepped up to support me in my journey in ways that were above and beyond anything I would have expected from any friend. Their involvement and their commitment to me was nothing short of miraculous, and I will never forget their generosity of spirit.

Lesson learned: Miracles can come in large or small packages. Rejoice in them all. They should never go unnoticed.

MIRACLES

Pay attention.
Miracles are all around you, like shiny pennies waiting to get picked up.
Be grateful for the abundance of daily miracles in your life,
even in your darkest days
Pay attention
to the love, kindness, and compassion which surrounds you
Miracles are there to nourish you on your journey.
Pay attention

Mercia Tapping

SUFFERING
April 5th, 2014

There are countless teachers of Eastern philosophy who will tell you that the greatest lessons in life are learned from suffering, and some would even say we should welcome suffering into our lives for that very reason.

As I look back on my own life, I can see many wonderful lessons that I learned from adversity, and then afterwards rising above it all. I grant you that there can be much learned by going through the burning fires of major life trials. I can attest to that. But I do not welcome suffering. Far from it. Yesterday, my friend Ann said, when we were reviewing the last five years of my life, "Enough already."

I do gain some comfort from believing that there is some divine plan to the life hurdles that we are given—a real life *Gulliver's Travels*. But I do not subscribe to either passively accepting suffering, welcoming it, wearing it as a mantle, succumbing to it, or on the other hand feeling victimized by it.

All the major events that have happened in my life in recent years have been very hard, and there is no doubt that I have suffered from either physical pain, or the grief of losing my beloved husband to brain cancer, and now my own fight for my life with breast cancer. But then the question becomes: *what do you do with the suffering after you have been through the worst of the fire?* My choice has always been to get up again, fight, and reflect on the life lessons that have been thrust on me.

I cannot tell you all the lessons that I am learning from being a breast cancer patient, as this is too soon in my journey. I CAN tell you that I have been touched to the very core of my being by the love and support expressed for me. I understand the commandment of "Love thy neighbor as thyself" in an entirely different way. Somehow, as the "Ace of Hearts" told me: this is all about love. Love is my protection, my guide and my reward.

The lessons from the suffering of being a caregiver of a spouse with brain cancer have forever changed me. I am not the same person anymore. I think all suffering does that. It changes you forever. It is then a choice as to which way it changes you. In the case of my experience with my husband's brain cancer, I learned far more compassion for the travails of the sick and the elderly. I also learned not to get upset by the insignificant and unimportant events that happen on a daily basis. I learned to rejoice and treasure the small things that made me smile each day. They are always there if you look hard enough. Those learnings have set me up to begin my own cancer journey from a different starting point. I am not even afraid of death, as I have looked death in the eye several times with loved ones.

After my husband's death, I did not feel impelled to share my journey as a widow or my retrospective musing of a caregiver, even though the cause of caregivers is close to my heart. But this time, with my current life challenge of breast cancer, I feel compelled to tell my story, in the hope that it will help those who come after me find the courage to face the hurdles that are set before them.

DIET AND EXERCISE
April 7th, 2014

Here is my diet and exercise story. I am 5'6 1/2" and weigh 135 pounds when I came to the USA some 40 years ago. Since then weight control has been an issue, and I have gone up and down all over the place from 126 to 250 pounds, many good slender years, and a few not so good years. I am clearly an emotional eater, who, in times past, did not control portions, grazed at night for comfort—although I might add, I have never been one to pig out on desserts. My goal is 165 pounds, which is the top of the healthy range for my height.

Caregiving for my husband put me over the edge to an all-time high of 250 pounds and I hated the way I looked, just hated it. I wanted to reclaim the beautiful woman that I knew I could be, but had lost. So, after his death in Fall 2011, I started attending a weight loss group for healthy eating and cooking, and was hovering around 200 pounds last Fall. I also started pilates on machines for toning. I felt that I was on the right track, although creeping along way too slowly, perhaps due to a sluggish thyroid (still to be determined). I logged my daily food intake for two years and counted calories or points. It was clear that I needed to shave off just a bit more each day and increase my activity level. No real mystery.

Then disaster hit with the news of my cancer and, what with holiday eating, and friends stuffing me with desserts over dinner at their houses, my weight was 203 pounds when I first got weighed at MGH (with clothes on) in early February. Now two months later it is 209.

I have been told not to diet and not to stress about it going through chemotherapy, and to be aware that steroids (Decadron) do not help, as one retains water and the Dex can make one ravenous. But a significant number of people gain 30-50 pounds while on chemotherapy. I think it is a combination of several factors, not the least of which is, when you are not feeling so well you look for food you can enjoy and actually eat (as opposed to grimacing and cannot swallow) and then eat too much of it. Right now, I eat several little meals.

I have two weight goals. One is to return to 200 pounds by the end of chemo (mid June), re-establish my sensible healthy eating, and continue with pilates. How much other exercise I can do remains to be seen, since I have surgeries and radiation in my future this year. But I cannot let my cancer be an excuse for losing control. I have fought too hard for this weight loss to just gain it all back. I have cut back on sugar already and my glucose levels are down. Now I need less carbs (bread, rice, pasta), although I do not intend to cut them out entirely. I want very much to be able to return to golfing and even tennis, which I used to love. However, walking may be all I can do this year.

FOOD
April 8th, 2014

I am a very good cook without reaching any dizzy heights of culinary excellence or presentation, such as you might see on a TV cooking show. As I have already mentioned, after Herman died I attended a healthy eating cooking school so that I could rediscover what I liked to cook and learn different eating habits, now that I was widowed. It was a delightful exploration, and a safe social activity.

Before I started chemotherapy, I went on a cooking frenzy, stocking my freezer up with pre-cooked meals and soups, since I knew I would have less energy for cooking while going through treatment. I wish I could say that it was a truly worthwhile activity. What I did not really count on was how my tastebuds were going to react, how bad some of my favorite foods were going to taste, and how my cravings were going to change on an almost daily basis. I never quite knew what I wanted to eat. I kept searching for ways to satisfy my tastebuds; sometimes I almost lucked out and enjoyed my food, especially if there was a sweeter edge to it. However, eating has been largely a miserable experience, and I gave away a lot of the food in my pantry and freezer. You would think that with food tasting not as good, let alone wine tasting like vinegar, that chemotherapy would be the best weight loss program on the planet. Strangely enough, as far as I can ascertain, many breast cancer patients gain weight, although a few do lose a couple of pounds. Whether it is the steroids or just comfort eating, I do not rightly know. But weight gain is common and I turned out to be no exception, although I struggled very hard to continue healthy eating. But truthfully, there were some days when even pulling something out of the freezer to microwave became too much effort, and takeout, even if it did not taste that great, was the more convenient option. My friends offered to cook meals for me and tempt my appetite. Occasionally, they scored a winner, but most of the time I politely ate their meals with no great relish. I finally understood that I was eating to live and not living to eat. Unfortunately, this was not a happy realization.

4th ROUND CHEMO
April 8th, 2014

I went today for my fourth round out of eight chemotherapy infusions. Amazing, I am at the halfway chemo mark. I can't say any of this is easy as I confront controlling numerous side effects, which I have a tendency to try to ignore. However, the doctors at MGH have been down this road before and have a bucket full of good advice. My chemotherapy regimen changes at the end of the month to every alternate week. The very good news is there will be a vastly decreased dose of the steroid, the main benefit of which is I should sleep better, and controlling neuropathy and weight will be easier to manage. What's more, if I seem to be coping with nausea pretty well, maybe the steroid can be eliminated entirely. I was almost doing a happy dance. In the meantime, my oncologist told me to take some ginseng to boost my energy, and admonished me yet again for stressing about gaining weight. He also said he would much rather be hearing that my business was increasing sales, instead of me being so stressed about the business.

The tumors continue to shrink and respond to treatment, and my blood work shows everything is holding up well. My liver and kidneys are holding steady and my glucose is way down, so yeah for me for cutting back on sugar! I had a surfeit of white blood cells when I began this process, meaning that I was as strong as a horse. Now I have lost one third of my white blood cell count, but am still top of the normal range. The next series of chemotherapy blasts will take a serious whack at me and the doctors will probably want to inject me each time with a white blood cell count booster at vast expense (several thousand dollars per shot) if my insurance will pay—TBD. Without the booster, I will be mega fatigued and my white blood cell count will be through the floor.

Next week, I go for a halfway mark consultation with Dr Kevin Hughes, the surgeon who heads my team. I have many, many questions for him since a mastectomy is the standard recommended procedure for my condition, followed by reconstruction. Neither operation is trivial. Far from it. This will be a very challenging conversation. I now realize why doctors do not lay it all out for you at once; it would be too much to handle. One step at a time. It is all you can handle.

ADVICE FROM AN ONCOLOGIST
April 10th, 2014

This anonymous post below, which I found online, really spoke to me as I have begun my breast cancer journey. There is a raw truth in it, and reading it made me cry. It was certainly true as my journey as a caregiver of my husband going through brain cancer.

"Your relationships are about to change.

All of them. Some will get stronger. They will probably not be with the people you would expect. The people you want to handle this well might not be able to for a variety of reasons. Some of the reasons will be selfish. Some of them will be entirely innocent and circumstantial. All of them will be forgivable because no one plans for cancer. Carrying bitterness or anger won't help your recovery. Fighting for anyone to stick with you won't cure you. Those who can, will.

You will be determined to have more energy than you do.

You will convince yourself that you are thinking straight, are able to handle all of this and do not need anyone. You will run out fuel. Your body will change first and your mind will follow. You won't lose your mind, memories or sensibility. It will all come back. But, you will be different. You will never have the same sense of self. You should embrace this. Your old self was probably really great. Your transformed self will be even better. Give in to what is happening and trust it.

You are going to feel fear.

Even if you are normally stubborn, confident and seemingly invincible you will finally find yourself admitting that you are scared of something. Cancer is scary and incredibly confusing. The unknown will eat at you worse than the disease itself. You'll need distractions. Music and sleep will probably be the ones you resort to most. Reading will become difficult. So will watching TV or movies, having conversations, writing and basically everything else. They call it "chemo brain" for a reason. You will feel normal eventually. Just a new kind of normal. When you feel afraid, let yourself lean on those around you. Cry. Be vulnerable. You are vulnerable. There will be time for strength, but never admitting weakness will cause anxiety to mount and your condition to worsen. Let it all out. Yell if you need to. Sing when you feel up to it. Sob uncontrollably. Apologize for your mood swings. Treatments and prescriptions will often be the cause of them. The people that love you will understand.

The people that love you will be just as scared as you are.

Probably more. They will be worrying even when they are smiling. They will assume you are in more pain than you are. They will be think-

ing about you dying and preparing for life without you. They will go through a process that you will never understand, just like they will never understand the process you are going through. Let them process. Forgive them when they don't understand. Exercise patience when you can. Know that those that were built for this will be there when you get to the other side, and you will all be able to laugh together again. You'll cry together too. Then you'll get to a place where you will just live in the world again together and that is when you know that you have beaten this.

The sooner you recognize that you are mortal, the sooner you can create the mentality for survival.

There is a chance you might not make it. Just like there is a chance that you will. Don't look at statistics. You are unique and what is happening inside you is unique. Your fight is yours alone and there are too many factors to compare yourself to others that have had your condition. No one will want you to think about death, but you won't have a choice. You will think about it from the moment you are given your diagnosis. Come to terms with it. Calmly accept it. Then, shift every thought you have into believing that you won't die. You are going to beat this. Your mental focus on that fact will be more powerful than any treatment you receive.

Your doctors and nurses will become your source of comfort.

You will feel safe with them. If you do not feel safe with them you need to change your care provider immediately. There is no time to waste. This shouldn't be a game played on anyone's terms but yours. When you find the right caretakers you will know immediately. Do not let insurance, money or red tape prevent you from getting the treatment you deserve. This is your only shot. There is always a way. Find those hands that you trust your life in and willingly give it to them. They will quickly bring you a sense of calm. They will spend time answering your questions. There will be no stupid questions to them. They won't do anything besides make you feel like you are the most important life that exists. They will never make you feel like they don't have things in control. They will be honest and accessible at all times. They might even become your friends.

You might celebrate with them over drinks months or years after they have cured you. They deserve your gratitude, respect and appreciation daily. If you get upset at them during treatment, know that they'll forgive you. They get that you're going through something they can't imagine—but they understand better than anyone. They see it every day and they choose to be there because they want to make the worst experience of your life more tolerable.

You will need to find balance after treatment.

Start by seeking balance during treatment. Eat well. Sleep well. Listen to your body. Explore meditation. Experiment with new forms of exercise that aren't so demanding. Embrace massage and other body therapies. Go to therapy. A therapist will be able to guide you through your journey in ways you could never fathom. Do not be too proud to speak to someone. You cannot afford to store up the intensity of the emotion that comes with fighting a life-threatening illness. Let it out for yourself. You will begin to hear your voice changing. That voice is who you are becoming in the face of mortality. Listen to that voice. It will be the purest, most authentic version of you that you have ever known. Bring that person into the world—strengths and vulnerabilities and everything between. Be that person forever.

You will inspire others. It will feel weird.

People you haven't spoken to since grade school will be in touch. Ex-girlfriends, former colleagues... even people you felt never wanted to talk to you again. The influx of interest in your seemingly fading life will be greater than any living moment you have ever experienced. That support is what will shift a fading life into a surviving one. Be grateful for every message. Be appreciative of each gift and each visit. There will be moments where all of this attention will make you feel lonelier than you have ever felt in your life. In a hospital room full of people with messages stuffing your inbox, voicemail and mailbox you will find yourself feeling completely alone. This is when you will realize that you could afford to have a stronger relationship with yourself. That only you walk this earth with 100% investment in you. Make the investment and use this as an opportunity to re examine your self-worth. Love yourself more than ever and recognize how much love there is for you in the world. Then start sharing that love. You will come to see that even when you are the neediest person you know you can still be giving. Giving will make you feel better than taking.

When you get to the other side you won't believe it.

They will tell you the disease is gone. Everyone you know will rejoice and return back to their lives. You'll constantly wonder if it is coming back. Slowly this feeling will fade, but cancer will always be a part of you. It will define how you see the world moving forward. You're going to feel like the future is a funny thing to think about because the present is going to suddenly seem incredibly important. Keep moving. You'll be more productive. You'll understand who truly loves you because they will still be there. You'll want to meet new people that connect to the newly evolved version of your old self. You'll want to let go of those that don't "get" who you are now. You'll feel a little guilty doing it. Then, you'll move on. You don't have time to waste. The greatest gift you've been given is that you now understand that and you're going to make the most of every second. You're going to be the most passionate person you know going forward. Translate that passion to a greater purpose. Be fearless again."

Author unknown

EVEN THE BRAVEST FEEL FEAR
April 15th, 2014

This is the eve of the halfway point consultation tomorrow with the head of my team, Kevin Hughes, a surgeon. It has slowly become clearer that even if I disappeared all visible cancer cells, that the recommended course of treatment for my grade of breast cancer is a mastectomy. A double mastectomy, if I carry the cancer gene. My oncologist said that although my tumors are shrinking nicely with the chemotherapy, if a decision had to be made today, it would be for a mastectomy, but to bear in mind it is a moving target. Ever since my mother's breast cancer and her mastectomy some 30 years ago, I have dreaded that one day I might follow her footsteps.

I am now struggling. Better than dying, you say? Easy for you to trip that off your tongue. My hair and my breasts have always been my crowning glory. Now I have no hair, and while I know it will grow back one day, nevertheless, an important part of me is just not there every day. And now I have to cope tomorrow with the thought of losing my lovely breasts. Just get reconstruction, you say—they do wonders nowadays. Still you do not understand. These are the beautiful ample breasts that Herman adored and were part of our lovemaking. They felt his love and caresses. And more likely they will be taken away from me and never feel another man's touch. And let's not forget that a mastectomy is major surgery and I will have terrible scars. Why should you be concerned about scars, you say? I was on the road to losing weight and restoring my body to a more slender and youthful look again, when overnight I have been reduced to a bald-headed old woman who is probably about to lose her breasts, that precious symbol of being female. That is why I weep and feel fear tonight. Even the bravest woman can wobble and feel the fear as it grips her throat like the noose of the hangman getting tighter and tighter. The end.

SETTING SUN

I sit and look at the setting of the sun,
And long to walk, if not run.
In my mind I walk proud and tall,
While in reality, I can hardly crawl,
As a bird I would fly so free
Or perhaps a boat, full sail at sea.
Please tell me what becomes of me,
And the secret to my recovery?
Right now, I truly do not know.

The phone rings, it is a friend at last
Who counsels, time now, forget the past
And try to go as best with flow.

I hear the words, all good advice
Please tell me twice,
and don't forget, repeat it thrice.

Friends tell me my future will clearly be,
One in which emerges a brand new me.
I hope indeed they are indeed all right
As this day journeys into night.

Mercia Tapping

TODAYS MIRACLE, TUMORS CONTINUE TO SHRINK
April 16th, 2014

Today I went to visit my surgeon, Kevin Hughes, exactly at the half-way mark through my chemotherapy regimen. Last night I was racked with fear and anxiety, finally admitting that even the bravest can feel fear. As far as I could ascertain anywhere, the most common recommendation for an advanced Stage 3, triple positive cancer, was going to be for a mastectomy. The anticipated loss of a breast, one of the symbols of my womanhood, has been intense, besides dreading the lifelong residue of discomfort that can sometimes occur after such a major surgery.

But the universe was smiling on me today. After examining me, the surgeon was grinning broadly as my tumors had dramatically shrunk in size. He then declared me to be a lumpectomy candidate, and I will have an operation in the middle of July. I start my new series of four A-C chemotherapy infusions at the end of April, every alternate week, ending early June. I know this next chemotherapy series is predicted to be tougher, as it can involve nausea and mouth sores, but now I can welcome them as a friend helping me avoid a mastectomy. A set of 33 radiation treatments will begin mid August, then will be followed by antibody infusions for nine months. It is a long haul.

MIRACLES ARE HUMBLING
April 17th, 2014

As Spring has been taking its first tremulous steps outside my windows, I have been looking out on those golfers who have rushed to joyously embrace the advent of the new season. I have been watching with a big lump in my throat, and tears have rolled down my face, as I sadly have come to realize that fatigue, and my treatments, will keep me otherwise occupied all golf season long. A gentle stroll around the block will more likely be my exercise than my customary whacking a golf ball with gay abandon.

So when the head pro of our golf club asked me yesterday if I was joining the golf club as a member this year, I had to explain why not. I told him that I was going to keep my golf gear in the car on the off chance that late one afternoon here and there when fatigue and treatments did not interfere, I might snatch a few holes and feel all was not lost. I was incredibly touched when he replied that I should come and play anytime as his guest. I am so humbled by people's kindness to me. I feel very small and inadequate in the face of the compassion people are showing me.

SMALL MIRACLES, I AM GRATEFUL
April 25th, 2014

Small miracles are fleeting and can fly by unnoticed if you are not conscious of them and jot them down. They are unexpected, but always bring a smile to my face.

Take the example of repairs to my glasses. The last time I went into Pearle Vision, where I have bought generations of eye glasses, was in February 2014, when I confessed that the glass on one side had fallen out during a hospital visit that day. Much to my surprise, I was told it could be covered by my damage insurance and would only cost $25 for the new lens. That was so much better than the figure than I had anticipated. It made me smile!

Imagine my embarrassment, just two months later, when my glasses went missing only to reappear with one side severely bent. I limped into Pearle Vision expecting the worst again, but asked if they could try to bend the side and straighten it out. A very obliging sales assistant did her best but cautioned that the glasses would probably not hold up. Then she asked whether I had eyeglass insurance. After checking my insurance, she said that it had run out three days beforehand but she would stretch the time limits, because she would feel better if I had a whole new pair of glasses. So some $45 later, which included an up-charge for more expensive frames, I was the proud owner of a brand new set of specs! See what I mean by the unexpected nature of miracles?

But there has been so much in the way of numerous small miracles. There are the people who bump into me at the store and tell me that I look beautiful. That always brings a smile to my face! I am truly incredulous at the number of people, some of whom I hardly know, who send me cards, flowers, fruit, and numerous small, thoughtful gifts. I never expect gifts, but I find it immensely touching that the sender went to all this trouble to show that they are thinking of me and wish me well. It just shows me the generosity and the better side of humanity. There is something incredibly humbling in what is happening and I am constantly choking back tears at people's kindness towards me. I am far more used to being a giver and taking care of others. Letting other people care for me is a mysterious and new experience.

Lesson learned: Miracles and love are there in abundance but it is like an unused muscle. You need to exercise it. Look around you, it is waiting for you.

IT'S NOT EASY
April 25th, 2014

I never expected this journey to be easy, but strange to say I never expected it to be this hard. If I take stock from head to toe, I am almost bald, with very few eyelashes and eyebrows, my eyes run constantly, I have nose bleeds, I am permanently congested, I drool, I have heart-burn, occasional nausea, neuropathy on my hands and feet, hemor-rhoids, and itching and pain in my private parts. And then of course, on top of it all, I am super fatigued. Nothing by itself is earth shatteringly painful, but put them all together and I just do not feel well. I truly try to focus on the glass that is half full, and the wonderful kindness that people have been showing me, but I am still human. Since I live alone, I can't help but think back to the days when my husband would have taken care of me and would have held my hand in bed at night. Now I have to tough it out alone, clinging to the belief that it is going to get better, yet knowing in four days that I will enter the most rugged period of my chemotherapy treatment. I think that is what is getting me down tonight. I am scared of this next chemotherapy phase coming up.

Lesson learned: I am human. I wobble. I get scared and that is okay. It is not a sign of weakness, just my humanity.

CAT PUKE
April 25th, 2014

I went downstairs to the lower level where Jon usually stays and I found that Truffles had thrown up everywhere. Jon is arriving in three days and my heart just sank. I have so little extra energy and every chore is a huge deal to accomplish. Worst still is that my trusty steam cleaner has gone missing and no one has owned up to having borrowed it.

Then today's miracle occurred. My friend Sandy had heard that I was besieged by cat puke and had no efficient way to clean it up. She told me that she would be passing quite close to my house and she would come with her steam cleaner to clean up for me and she did just that. She blew into clean, then quickly left again to look after her Alzheimer's husband. That is one amazing friend. She just knew how I would be fretting. Instant relief.

Every day, I look at my list of what I would like to accomplish in the way of chores, and every day I fall short of my target. I am becoming the queen of naps and I do not like it. So when Sandy does my carpet stains, or the handyman changes my light bulbs, it just puts a little bit of order back into my world. And that makes me smile.

Lesson learned: True friends reach out and help you in amazing ways and the best of them do not ask how they can help, they just do it.

WIGS GONE WILD
April 27th, 2014

I bought a new wig at the wig store today. Definitely today's miracle, as this wig is the right color and fit. It needs trimming by my hairdresser, but I think it will turn out really nicely.

The staff at the wig store even said my hair was growing curly. Only something that I have wanted my entire life—curly hair! I gather it will stay curly for about a year or so before it turns back to normal. But it is very grey; I can do without looking at the grey as it truly makes me feel old. In the meantime, I will have a wig wardrobe because it is going to take the best part of two years to grow my hair. The wigs actually look really good and truly are convenient—just shake them out and away you go. But what everyone says about wigs being hot and uncomfortable is true. The moment I am alone, in the house or car, the wig comes right off. But at least when I see myself in a wig, I can see the beautiful woman again. And that, my friends, is a big relief.

Lesson learned: I am still a beautiful woman despite my hair loss. That woman is not lost forever.

5th CHEMO INFUSION
April 29th, 2014

I had the first of the final five chemotherapy infusions yesterday, which are the ones predicted to be more rugged. That is, as they say, an understatement. I can confirm firsthand that the ugly rumors you might have heard about the side effects of the "Red Devil" are absolutely true. I had intense nausea all night and vomited this morning three times. At some point, I wasn't sure of how much more I could take since it was so bad. The first five days are reputed to be the worst, then I will hopefully pick up a bit. Thankfully, the anti-nausea medication, which MGH had to write a letter of medical necessity to my insurance company for, is starting to keep things semi under control. I keep telling myself that this is helping to shrink tumors so I can avoid a mastectomy, and if I lose a few pounds in the process to offset the few that I have gained in the first half of my treatment, then here lies a silver lining. Only two months more and this part of my treatment will be over.

Jon is here this week helping look after my business and was very sweet and caring last night as I was wobbling after returning from my infusion. Despite my loving his company, I had to excuse myself at 8pm to go and lie down, after forcing down a little dinner. However, he was optimistic that we might be seeing little chinks of light at the business, and that all is not lost. It will get easier when we are no longer funding the newly imposed Bank of America reserve on a daily basis. 25% of daily sales carved off to fund a new reserve is very punitive.

THE RED DEVIL

I watch helplessly as the Red Devil slowly invades my body.
I try to welcome it as a life saving visitor.
But the truth is fear, fear grips my throat and every fiber of my body.
I am being poisoned and my body knows it.
This brutish treatment attacks every part of me with relentless imprecision.
I stagger to my bedroom window and look to the sky and whisper
"Dear God, please deliver me from my suffering."

Mercia Tapping

MAY IS BRAIN CANCER MONTH
May 1st, 2014

May 1st, and the month of brain cancer awareness. I gave up almost two and a half agonizing years of my life to Glioblastoma and the grieving as a widow has taken far longer than anticipated. Yet the unexpected fight for my own life with breast cancer has pushed active grieving to one side. Turning around my own health and that of my business is all I have room for right now. Still, tonight I turn my mind back to exactly five years ago, when I would have told you that I lived a charmed life, before the nightmare of not one, but now two cancers began. I had a man in my life who loved me unconditionally; it was a blessing and a gift I will never forget. And I know he watches me still from Heaven. I know I cannot have my old life back, and I know that at the end of my cancer journey my life will belong to the world. It is not about me. But on this day of remembrance, I honor him.

NOT A COMPETITION
May 2nd, 2014

A few of my brain cancer warrior sisters are angry that brain cancer gets so little publicity compared to breast cancer. I will be forever identified with my brain cancer caregiver sisters. We have shared a journey of incalculable pain and loss. I actually think it is easier fighting for one's own life than watching helplessly as one's spouse slowly but surely succumbs to this horrific disease. I know that when scientists have finally tamed this beast, I will shed tears of joy, despite it being too late for my beloved Herman. Several of those I know who have lost loved ones to brain cancer raise money for research and work tirelessly for brain cancer publicity. I could not applaud those efforts more loudly. But remember not to be angry that breast cancer has received more publicity to date. This is not a competition between grey and pink, or any other color for that matter. All cancer and the pain it brings to our lives is to be despised. I would also include a number of the terminal neurological diseases. What is true, is that apart from love, when you have your health, you have the most important thing in life, and to take it away is to suffer. The promoters of breast cancer awareness have blazed a trail in showing us that the public's awareness and scientific funding can be increased. That is a phenomenal achievement. Brain cancer advocates just need to follow suit. We need compassion for all cancer patients, and I for one am grateful for the compassion that is being shown for my breast cancer journey, which—and this may surprise you—is being most strongly shown to me by my "grey sisters." I have always said that my journey as a brain cancer caregiver has made me so much more compassionate to the sick and elderly. Today, I salute the ladies who wear grey in brain cancer memoriam.

ABOUT LOVE
May 2nd, 2014

There are numerous times on this journey where I have begun to realize that it is all about love, giving it freely to those around you and beyond, and learning to let others love you. I continue to be constantly amazed at the number of people who have said they are inspired by me, see me as a role model, or as a rock of strength in times of adversity. And the outpouring of loving gestures and assistance offered to me during my breast cancer journey is humbling.

One thing my friend Jon said this week rather disturbed me. He said marriage always ends in tragedy: divorce or death. Of course, in one sense that is absolutely true. I knew when I married Herman, who was some ten years older than myself, that chances were I would one day be widowed. But I do believe it is better to have loved in the in-between. Walling oneself off from love for the fear of getting hurt, rejected or widowed is to cast aside the greatest gift we have to give each other. And any time we take the risk to love another human being, we run the risk of it not being returned or it ending prematurely.

When I have finished my breast cancer journey, I do intend to find another life partner; this would make me profoundly happy. I have been very happy before and think I can be so again.

TRUST IN THE COCOON
May 4th, 2014

As I irrevocably slip deeper and deeper into the cocoon, it becomes harder and harder to trust that there is a divine plan and it will all work out the way it should in the end. Going into this journey, I would have told you that with the right level of intentionality, you can have anything you want—just put your mind to it. I have always believed in the power of positive thinking. Yet there is a gnawing and haunting reality that whispers in the back of my mind: you do not always get what you want, however intentional you are. After all, what person in their right mind signs up for their husband to die of brain cancer, for their very successful business to struggle for survival, and to contract advanced aggressive breast cancer? Life happens and it sometimes sends you curveballs.

So I sit here in the cocoon wondering where the lemonade is to be made of all these lemons. What is the divine purpose and life's lesson for all of this pain and suffering? Somewhere deep inside I feel there is a command to find my voice and inspire others. But here, deep in the cocoon, feeling mildly nauseous, and glumly and dutifully picking up a spoon to eat my breakfast of yoghurt and fruit, being inspirational and educating others seems a very far off goal.

As a type A kind of gal, coming to peace with the fact that I am in this transitional cocoon is not easy. I wish a hundred times over each day to just be given a glimpse of the future to give me the hope and the strength to continue. I can endure anything if I only I knew it would have a happy ending. And my happy ending? Oh, that is easy enough. I would have turned around my business with Jon's help and sold it to a company who have the deep pockets to allow it to grow again, which would allow me the financial security to enjoy the next chapter of my life. Of course I would be healthy again, swinging my golf clubs, traveling the world, and even venturing out on a tennis court once more. Naturally, I would be secure and happy, basking in the love of a new male partner in life.

Lesson learned: You are where you are at even if it is deep within the cocoon. Even a cocoon does not last forever. Remember that.

THE CANCER CLOUD
May 5th, 2014

When I began this breast cancer journey, I declared that cancer was not going to dominate my life. It was simply going to be a minor inconvenience in the background while I went on with my life as normal. Words bravely spoken, but cancer has a habit of inserting itself into every fiber of your being. You constantly have reminders, whether big or small, that you are just not healthy. You slow down, most food is unappetizing, your brain clouds over, and you monitor a sackful of side effects. Without realizing it, you withdraw from social life and chalk off each day as being nearer the end of chemotherapy. You wake up to the reality of cancer each morning, to the terror of cancer, and question where your life is going in the middle of the night. Cancer is that uninvited guest that barges in and disturbs the peace. There is no doubt that cancer has disturbed my peace and indeed my joy in life. I think of myself as in a cocoon, and have faith that the butterfly will emerge once more and joyously fly free. But for now my life as I knew it is in suspense. I wish I could tell you otherwise, and that I was able to cast off the mantle of cancer with brave abandon, but it is far harder than that. It is a battle for my body and mind and I have to get up and fight for my health each and every day.

Lesson learned: I began my cancer journey by saying that it would not be the focus or dominate my life. Words bravely spoken, but in my case unrealistic. I fight the daily fight and there is no shame in admitting that it is a fight.

THE CHEMO PRAYER

When will I rise to smell the flowers,
Instead of simply counting hours?
I greet each day with dark and gloom.
Deliverance seems no time soon.
My mind struggles to lift itself above the fray,
I search for happy thoughts to rule the day.
That is surely a great stretch,
When often all I do is wretch.
Yet little chinks of light,
Tell me an end's in sight.
I believe there is a season
Even though in suffering I find no reason.
So with courage I rise out of bed,
And choose life, tis better than dead.

Mercia Tapping

HOW HARD DO YOU FIGHT?
May 5th, 2014

At some point in the cancer journey, you are faced with the reality of your own mortality. Everybody has to die sometime, so how much do you want to live?

I always envied those with husbands, children and grandchildren, because that will to live for them would seem, at least to me as an outsider, to be built in or at least inherently stronger than those of us who are single. In my own case, I had none of these built-in incentives to live. I have one sister whom I adore, but who lives 3000 miles away in England, and despite our being close through weekly Facetime calls, she has her own life to lead. My sister and my niece Ann did in fact make a flying visit to see me for a 4-day visit back in March. It was a treat and I wished we lived closer.

My life as I had known it in the last few years has gradually fallen apart. In 2009 I became a caregiver to my husband dying of brain cancer, and after his death in 2011 I had scarcely recovered before in 2012 discovering that my company was on the brink of financial ruin, because of the ill-advised cooking of the books by my CFO. Only a few months later, I was diagnosed with stage 3 breast cancer and learned it had spread, although not mestasticized, to major organs. I have looked around my house, my home and little castle. I do not want to lose it. I had lost one home before in my career, due to my entrepreneurial ups and downs. I do not want a repeat performance. I am afraid that if I lost my home, I would then discover my breaking point. Everyone expects you to fight and kick cancer's ass, but it wasn't quite so automatic as you might think with me. It wasn't that I wanted to commit suicide; remnants of a Catholic upbringing would preclude that option, but the fight for my health has stretched out in front of me in ways that have been very unappealing. It is going to be a long journey and has already proved to be very arduous at times. The more I have discovered about chemo, surgery, radiation and hormone treatment, the less appealing and more frightening it all has become. Sometimes I have doubted whether I had the fortitude to fight for my own life and that of my business at the same time. And for what at the end of it? There were moments that joining Herman in Heaven held more appeal than you might realize. I am not afraid of death, having stared it in the face several times, with both parents and my husband. It was and is the actual process of dying that I fear, as terminal illnesses hold nothing redemptive in my opinion. Being ill sucks. But if someone had said to me that I could click my fingers and join my husband in Heaven, I might well have taken that option. But since that option does not exist, I have had to find a reason to fight for my life. Strangely enough I had to look outwards rather than inwards to find the answers.

No one can give you the will to live, and there are many who have witnessed my journey up close who have said they do not think they would have had the courage to go through chemotherapy, especially with no children or grandchildren giving them some inbuilt purpose to live. All I can say is, you never know what you are going to do until that choice is put in front of you. For me, it was my spiritual connection with the afterlife and my belief in a divine being that gave me some sense that it wasn't my time to leave this planet yet; there was something, still concealed, that I was supposed to contribute to the world. Sometimes, I might get some glimpses into that future, but for the most part the intensity of the misery of the chemotherapy journey has kept me rooted in the present.

My friend Jon has been fond of saying that the value of a life is measured in the love that a person leaves behind. A wallflower at a girls' boarding school in my youth, I never considered myself one to win any popularity contest. I have always been pathetically shy in a group of strangers. Of course, as an adult I have learned to hide my shyness better than during my youth, but I am not like Herman whose presence and voice used to light up a room upon entry. I have been one of those people who others exclaim with surprise, "Oh, she is so funny and nice when you get to know her!" As I said, I am an acquired taste. Nevertheless, and forgive me if this sounds sappy, but I have always tried to live by the golden rule and do my best by other human beings. I have tried my utmost to give others the respect and love I thought they deserved. Like in anybody's life, I have had my share of failures, but it was never for the lack of trying. If you look at the continuous thread throughout my life, it has been to champion the health, wellbeing and happiness of others. That purpose is something I have felt very deeply. But I have never felt especially loved by others. My journey through two cancer wars was about to change this.

There were those few friends with whom I could confide the pain, the terror and fatigue of living with a man dying of brain cancer. But for the most part, I hid that pain from the outside world. I tried hard to make every day of Herman's life count and filled with joy, but the truth is much of it was done through gritted teeth. The man whom I adored and who loved me unconditionally was gone from the moment he had his brain operation. He was never the same.

It was in the last few weeks of his life, sitting vigil at the hospice, that I was astonished at the love shown to me by my community. Perfect strangers had shown up at my door with meals, the men in the community had rushed to pick up Herman when he had fallen in the house, and I had sobbed in the arms of people I hardly knew. Little did I know I was finally letting myself be loved by those who were only waiting to be asked. I was incredulous at the outpouring of compassion for me and I felt blessed. Again, I was surprised at the number of people who came to his funeral in support of me. Former employees flew in from around the country. I felt so filled up with love that day as I looked out on all the people at Herman's funeral service and when I got up and gave his eulogy, it was not to ask for condolences but congratulations for a love that was well lived.

It was a couple of months later that my healing as a newly minted widow of brain cancer was about to progress in a most unexpected way. It was through Facebook, a medium that I had previously somewhat despised.

I found a secret group of women on Facebook who were either caregivers of a loved one with brain cancer, or were grieving the loss of their loved ones. As this courageous group of women voiced their most inner pain with incredible candor, I began to see that even my darkest thoughts and feelings during my husband's illness had also been felt by numerous others. It helped assuage my guilt and confusion. I began to heal and feel incredibly close to the women in this group, and was able to give back to others who were not so far along in their journey. In early 2012 some of the group members voiced that it would be wonderful to meet each other in person. CEO that I am, I said: "No problem, I will sponsor a retreat here at Pinehills and you can all stay with my friends." So that is precisely what happened in July 2012. Sixteen women flew in from all over the country for a three and a half-day retreat. Limos greeted them at the airport and my generous friends opened their doors to them and gave them beds for the duration of the retreat. I had organized massages, angel card readings, manicures and tourist activities in Plymouth. I had been cooking like a crazy woman for days, and a friend generously hosted a farewell BBQ around her pool. One of the surprise events that final night was a raffle of some clearance and return items from my company. So everyone went home with an assortment of air purifiers, hypoallergenic bedding and vacuum cleaners. It was a weekend full of tears, hugs and a great deal of laughter. It is a weekend I will never forget. The remarkable thing is that this retreat encouraged others all around the country to sponsor meet ups, and before long I was flying around to reconnect with existing friends and meet new ones. As we returned home and to our private Facebook page, my connectivity to these women only increased.

If I had to face my illness completely alone, it would have made it so much tougher to choose to live. I am not sure I would have been able to do it. But somehow there were others, many others, gently pulling me along. They all reminded me that I have so much still to give the world. Of course, when you are submerged in one's own pain, it is hard to see beyond it. But the first step is to choose to live, to choose to fight. And only you can make that choice.

Lesson learned: Choosing to live and to fight is a conscious decision, but it's easier to make when you are surrounded by friends rooting for you every step of the way.

WOO HOO
May 6th, 2014

I have ankles again and am not all bloated, since the previous series of chemotherapy meds are leaving my body. I hate fat ankles! This evening my girlfriend Linda is taking me out to a fish restaurant. I am so sick of these four walls at home and am going to take the chance of being out in public. A nice clean and ultra-fresh, straight from the boats each day, fish dinner will probably agree with my stomach pretty nicely, and my motivation to cook when I am by myself is slim to none.

ROLLER COASTER
May 9th, 2014

What a roller coaster this journey has become in so many different dimensions. One moment I am throwing up, feeling nauseous, and losing weight and the next moment I am eating like a horse! I never know what food I will want or crave and some of my food choices include things that I rarely, if ever, have eaten before.

My mood also is so up and down, which is such an anathema to a steady-Eddie type of person like myself. One moment I am feeling courageous and strong, and the next I am sitting in dread of my next infusion. I try very hard to count my blessings and find those silver linings. When people ask me how I am doing, I tell them, "Good, given the circumstances, and other people have worse side effects than I am encountering." It's all true, and my well wishers go away relieved and satisfied. But nobody in their right mind joyously anticipates their next infusion. Mine is four days away and, make no mistake, I dread it and it would be a real drag on my mood if I let it take hold. That is the built-in struggle, acknowledging that I have these more gloomy thoughts and then hauling myself up by my mental bootstraps and consciously turning the mind to my blessings and the good stuff happening in my life. So I am lucky; the next four nights are all spent dining with good friends, all part of my core support team. They are all people who accept me in the place I am now and are rooting for me coming out the other side. I am truly blessed to have a strong a support network. I know not everyone can say this.

GIFTS
May 10th, 2014

I have never been one to place much importance on receiving gifts, although I have been known to go completely overboard in spoiling those closest to me with wildly extravagant gifts and I enjoy locating that thoughtful little gift for a good friend. But, except for my husband who was duty bound to give me a birthday gift, I never looked or expected others to give me gifts. It just never occurred to me. I have to say that I have been deeply touched and surprised by the number of gifts that have been sent to me, many of which are from Facebook friends. I treasure them all, as they are so symbolic of the outpouring of love that has been shown to me. Even if it is something that is not my taste, I look at the object and I can feel the love behind it. It makes me ashamed of the callousness of my youth when I got angry at my mother for buying me the "wrong thing." The phrase "it is the thought that counts" is a well-worn expression that I have never dwelt upon. But now my house has many reminders of loving thoughts for me, of people who went out of their way to buy something and even went to the trouble of mailing something to me. This is part of my journey in learning to receive, and yet again I am humbled by the goodness in humanity.

Lesson learned: Allowing myself to be given to by others, by their deeds and gifts, is allowing them their joy of giving, which I have always felt when I give to others.

LAST NIGHT AND TODAY'S MIRACLE
May 13th, 2014

Yesterday, I declared a moratorium on cooking for the next few weeks. The thought of cooking is beyond me. This round of chemotherapy infusions has laid me almost flat with fatigue. Time to eat down my freezer. Today I was thanking Jan (who was subbing for Linda to drive me to my infusion) for the leftovers from the charity event on Saturday, which were quite astonishingly delicious and were so appreciated by Jon and myself.

Lesson learned: Miracles happen when you are least expecting them.

6th CHEMO AND FIGHTING STRONG
May 14th, 2014

Yesterday marked my sixth chemo infusion out of eight, and halfway through a series of four infusions of chemo, which includes a chemo with the rather appropriate nickname of the "Red Devil." I am pleased to announce that with the increased anti-nausea medication I slept well last night and avoided the brutality of the first night two weeks ago. Of course, if I made an inventory of annoying chemotherapy side effects that I cope with on a daily basis, I could deem myself a "hot mess." But I see no value in doing so and giving cancer any more air time than I find unavoidable. I can't deny that I have become the "Nap Queen," as the fatigue can be overwhelming at times, but I am not suffering from many other predictable very nasty side effects. The others, the residuals from the first four rounds of different chemo concoctions, are improving. On a very vain note, my poor hair is already making valiant attempts to grow, so I may never be completely bald, and right now I am already sprouting about two inches of chemo curls. By Christmas I may look like Annie!

Lesson learned: By the way, despite my hopes, I did later become completely and utterly bald, with not even a wisp of hair on my head.

MY BIG ANGEL
May 17th, 2014

There is no doubt that the biggest angel in my life, supporting me in my journey, is Jon Rivers. What a tower of strength and wisdom he is to me! He was slaying dragons at work all week in a highly focused effort to turn the business around for me. Just going and tackling issues head on where angels fear to tread. I am learning so much from him and know I am just far too tired right now to drive the company to success. Given how brilliant Jon is at business, I doubt I could ever do what he is doing. It is humbling to watch him at work. I am so profoundly grateful to him.

He is also so caring and supportive on the home front, encouraging me to eat by being around and cooking with me. Left to my own devices, I would not eat much during the first week of chemotherapy, and he makes sure that I keep my strength up and is a superior cook to me. I have never ceded the kitchen to a man, but he clearly is a very accomplished cook, with a refined palate. He expressed his concern last night that, left alone next chemo round when he can't be here, I won't eat so much. He is right, I won't. I did tell him I had a freezer full of food to eat down, but he astutely commented that this wasn't his concern, it was whether I would actually eat it.

I love to listen to him talk about his cooking acumen, as he tells me about how he will bake me some out of this world, exotic sounding fruit tarts this summer and decorate salads with edible flowers. It reminds me of my mother, who took cooking to an art form. I am sure Jon talks like this partially to stimulate my appetite during these first few post chemotherapy days. Smart strategy! Of course, with compromised tastebuds, nothing really tastes that great, but I truly am not worried about losing weight. If anything my weight is up three pounds since chemotherapy began.

I have never had a man take care of me when I was sick. It is a very new experience for me to allow others, let alone a man, to take care of me. Jon is very observant and notices when I am tiring and is just endlessly considerate. I got up this morning to find out that he had emptied the dishwasher at 5am before he left. It is the small things that count so much and make the difference.

MEMORIAL DAY
May 26th, 2014

It is the day before infusion #7 and yet again I woke up to a queasy stomach. As you can imagine, I am not exactly jumping up and down with joy at the prospect of chemotherapy tomorrow. At this point I have lost sight of what it means to feel normal, let alone well. Last week, a well-meaning health conscious friend invited me out for a walk. She has no clue of what it means to be a chemotherapy patient. My walks are confined to wobbling around my garden, and I am out of breath just walking from one end of the house to the other. A technician at MGH told me last week that some people are no longer even standing at this point in their treatment. I am still standing and fighting, perhaps not as strong as before, but still standing.

I keep reminding myself that I have less than one more month to go, and then I will be done with this phase of my treatment. I am luckier than some, and have avoided a number of nasty side effects. But make no mistake, I have a fistful of other very uncomfortable ones that require ministration several times a day to soothe the pain and discomfort. I will be so ready to see the back of chemotherapy.

Today is all about finishing all the chores I have to nail down before the next round of chemotherapy begins. There is no avoiding them. My greatest accomplishment this weekend, amply aided and abetted by others (read they were doing all the hard work), has been to have my new deck furniture assembled and my annuals planted in pots and window boxes. I decided that if I have to languish a bit this summer, I could at the very least design my annuals so that I can enjoy them from whatever window I look out from at the rear of my house. The new furniture is really easy to maintain, and anything that has the adjective "easy" in front of it makes it in my book right now.

Another thing I keep reminding myself about when I count my blessings, is that this last week my surgeon confirmed that I can have a lumpectomy and lymph node removal. This is scheduled for early July. It could have been far worse, and as long as clear margins are achieved, I can avoid a mastectomy and all that it entails.

There is also an expression "it takes a village"; my biggest blessing is the large team of friends who keep me going every step of the way, and their love and generosity never continues to amaze me.

I will limp rather than dance over the chemotherapy finish line in June. But I will get there. At this point, my chores await...

Lesson learned: One foot in front of the other, sometimes it is all you can do.

LET ME BE CLEAR
June 2nd, 2014

Let me be clear, in case anyone is in any doubt about this: these last few days of chemotherapy are lining up to be pretty brutal. I have lost sight of what it feels to be anywhere close to normal. Up till this point, I have tried to carry on my life as best as possible, but now the treatment process has bested me. For the last six days, I think I have slept the best part of 20 hours a day, getting up only to force a bit of food down on a queasy stomach. A bad UTI for three months certainly has not helped matters. The fatigue is beyond belief—who knew that anyone could want to sleep so much? I am not sure that I will be able to make it into work until my last infusion, on June 10th, has worked itself through my system. That does not make me happy, but my body gives me no choice.

I look at the golfers passing by my living room window in the sunshine. How I long to be out there with them instead of napping with darkened shades and tears rolling down my face. I know I am near the end of chemotherapy, and thank goodness, as I am not sure how much more of this I can take. I am just holding on by a thread to crawl over the finish line.

THE LOST SUMMER

Summer is so fleeting and the flowers bloom
So why indoors and feel the gloom?
My body hurts beyond belief,
I pray for when I see relief.
The tears trickle down my face with fear,
Dear God, please grant me another year.

Mercia Tapping

GROUNDHOG
June 5th, 2014

Somebody yesterday called me a groundhog because, after nine days post chemotherapy, I said I was just coming up for air. This next-to-last round of chemotherapy has been, predictably, very rough, challenging me to the brink of desperation. So I will share with you my chemo "wisdom."

1. Every diet under the sun amounts to eating fewer calories to lose weight. I can now testify that it is true.
2. In order to feel more comfortable, I drive around bald-headed, with my last remaining eyelashes making Custer's Last Stand. I comfort myself that no one would ever recognize me, and I pop on a wig before getting out of the car.
3. The best hydrating skin care is coconut oil and I smell like a Piña Colada for a few minutes, evoking happy beach-side memories.
4. Speak to me during chemo week, especially when I told you not to call, and my social filters will have vanished, giving me a preview that I could become a crabby old lady.
5. If Truffles, one of my Siamese, treads over my port (no, I do not mean the drink) as he exits the king-size bed multiple times during the night, or nibbles those teeny hairs on my head one more time, I will switch sides of the bed and confuse the poor cat and be accused of animal cruelty.
6. One of the advantages of being almost entirely hairless is my skin is very smooth and silky. But touch me and I will scream.
7. Being hairless means vast savings in hairdresser and waxing bills. Of course, I spend a small fortune at CVS where, as of this week, I am a proud card holder of the frequent prescription customer bonus plan, where I get an extra five bucks off for every ten prescriptions filled.
8. Given my tastebuds have changed, my dining out bills are minimal, and I have become one of those annoying people who asks if

they can eat dinner by just taking a little of your dinner onto my side plate.

9. Instead of worrying every time I have a memory lapse. I now have an excuse: "chemo brain," which I am told can last for years.

10. At least during chemo I can wear my nice form-fitting T-shirts. Rumor has it that after surgery I might have to "swing free" for a while. Lopsided and swinging free will require the floppiest tops I can find.

11. There are some splat marks on my sliding glass doors. These have been made by unsuspecting birds who have been frightened to death when they catch sight of the bald-headed wonder that lies within. I do not think I should go out on Halloween; I could be accused of child manslaughter.

12. Truffles is becoming visibly porky during my chemo months. He complains he needs to be fed and I can't remember if I did or not. He has become a very accomplished feline liar.

13. I have turned off the news on my TV, and am blissfully ignorant now of everything negative in the world. Who knew that ignorance was really bliss?

So that, my friends, is wisdom from Chemo Land.

Lesson learned: Keeping one's sense of humor, even in the darkest of days, is one of the ways to cling to the ropes of sanity.

IN THE DOMAIN OF LOVE AND MIRACLES
June 5th, 2014

I have been pondering all week about a rather amazing miracle. Jon and I were Skyping, primarily about business matters, when he rechecked the date of my upcoming surgery, which is Friday, July 11th. Then he informed me that he would like to come into Boston the day before the surgery and take me to the hospital (which means getting up before 4am) and he would collect me the next day and look after me post-surgery during the weekend. Then, after the weekend, he would stay during the week to run the business for me. I was so astonished at his offer that I broke down in tears. His caring and compassion never cease to amaze me.

It has made me think, yet again, that this journey is all about love. I never felt particularly lovable when I was growing up, and certainly did not win the popularity contest at my girls' convent boarding school. I evolved into someone who always tried to do my best for the rest of humanity, educating and inspiring others to better and healthier lives, but I always felt like a slight oddball, and moving from my native England did not help matters. I have always spoken with a British accent. So when Herman was suffering from brain cancer and said, "You had better try to keep me around, Honey, I am all you have got," his words had an icy ring of truth to them. Who would love me when he was gone? I understood why such a large number of people came to his funeral and Celebration of Life; he was a larger than life character with a very big heart—everyone loved him. But for me, I had put in my will that I was to be buried with no fanfare and no funeral. Why bother to have a funeral that no one would attend? Certainly not my sister, 3000 miles away. So I purchased a plot next door to Herman with a marker waiting with my name on it. No need to cause anyone any future trouble or expense.

But my journey with cancer has interrupted a long-held belief. When it started, I characteristically told my close friends I would be fine, that I could look after myself and not to worry about me. But the word of my illness spread. A veritable avalanche of letters, emails, cards, gifts, flowers, errands run, food cooked for me, has kept coming and coming. Even offers from people willing to cut off their hair for me to make a wig. People ignored the "I am fine." They insisted on driving me to infusions and courageously watched as the chemicals were being pumped into me, knowing that in a few hours I would be feeling as sick as a dog. They sat in doctors' offices with me and helped me sort out what the doctor was saying, and Jon offered to come in regularly to Boston to help turn around my business. They expressed their love, compassion and admiration of me. It has humbled me and opened my heart to receive love in a way I would have never predicted or thought possible.

CHEMO BRAIN TALKING
June 6th, 2014

Thankfully for most of you, you will never know what really goes on in a chemotherapy patient's mind, and their darkest thoughts, feelings and frustrations. In my case, I did not want to give these negative thoughts any more reality than a passing dot flitting through my brain. But I am sharing some of those inner agonizing thoughts with you so that you can appreciate that, while the rest of the world has seen someone who was facing chemotherapy with grace, wit and courage, nevertheless a ferocious battle for my spirit and mind was being fought each and every day. You can be sure that anyone who endures chemotherapy is having many of these same unvoiced thoughts.

- Five months of chemo? You have to be kidding me! That is five months of feeling sick.
- Don't tell me that breast cancer patients wear their bald heads as a symbol of courage. I loved my hair and the bald-headed woman in the mirror looks like a 90-year-old monster.
- If you tell me one more time how good I look, I will whip off my wig and show you reality.
- I really mean it about not calling me. Yet again, you have woken me up.
- If you suggest one more time that I can combat chemo with a green smoothie or a brisk hour-long walk, I will smack you. Don't you realize that I can hardly walk across the room?
- I have told you repeatedly that cancer cells feed off sugar, and I could have permanent neuropathy and diabetes if I do not cut down on sugar. So why tell me are you ignoring this information and serving me up dessert? Do you want to kill me?

- It was a lovely dinner, and I know you tried hard. Now I am going home to puke.
- What do you mean "think it over"? Don't you know that I cannot think?
- I do not want to be organized. It reminds me of my mother.
- I am puffed out walking across the room. This is ridiculous!
- Where is the remote? I have lost the remote! OMG it is in my hand, stupid!
- I put an egg out to cook for breakfast, where the heck is it? Things cannot vanish. No they don't, I just chucked a whole egg into the trash.
- I totally understand why people give up and just want to go to Heaven. This sucks.
- I can't read. Not enough concentration. So I will just sit here and listen to music like a big bump on a log.
- I am not interested in the news. I simply do not care about suffering in the rest of the world. Sad but true.
- When will food ever taste good again?
- Sex? Can't even muster an erotic dream. Feeling as dead as a dodo, and with a UTI. Touch me and I will hit you.
- Some CEO you are, napping on the office couch again.
- My driving skills have fallen off a cliff. It is the slow lane for you, girl. I hope my driving recovers one day.
- After chemo, it is still another whole year of treatment. What a marathon.

This, and much more, would flit through my brain as I slowly lost sight of what it was to be well. I do not believe that a chemotherapy patient can avoid these thoughts if they are in any way human. I would let these thoughts emerge, and then simply turn my attention elsewhere. Turning my attention elsewhere became more and more difficult as the chemotherapy months rolled on, but I knew that wallowing in misery was not productive. Somewhere in all this there was a reason for my suffering, some purpose for the rest of my life. And it surely wasn't to be found in these dark thoughts. But make no mistake. I certainly had them.

TIPS FOR MANAGING WEIGHT THROUGH CHEMO
June 10th, 2014

In the first few months of chemotherapy, despite some initial tastebud changes and difficulty swallowing, my appetite held up very well—too well. The steroids were doing their job, and a few days after each infusion I was ravenous and my weight began the slow upward creep. It never got beyond a six-pound gain, but to me this was the beginning of a very ominous end. Fortunately, all that diet and exercise chit chat in my Facebook group was very helpful.

The final few chemotherapy infusions with the different medicine were a natural appetite suppressant, so it was not entirely surprising, although very welcome, that the pounds that I had gained in the first three months of chemotherapy dropped back pretty effortlessly, and ended close to where I had started. However, there were some observations and simple learnings that I made along the chemotherapy journey that I hope stick with me for the rest of my life, and I will share them with you.

1.   Every diet under the sun recommends a reduction of caloric intake. It is all a question of which way you choose to reduce calories. Hopefully, you will choose a healthy way of eating that becomes habitual for a lifetime. I discovered, as I looked at my food log, that my caloric intake was within the boundaries that Weight Watchers recommend for losing weight. Losing weight is not as mysterious as you might think. It is the focus and will power that is the challenge.

2.   For many years, I have eaten what others would view as being pretty healthy, with minimal sugar or processed foods and plenty of fish, vegetables or fruit. The trouble is that you can eat too much of a

good thing. As I put less volume into my stomach, I could actually feel the skin shrinking and tightening, especially around the whale of my belly. So I do not think that eating very large volumes of low calorie food is the answer. I have always noticed that my thin friends just eat less volume than I do. Now I have become content with my meals fitting on salad plates. Anything more in volume and I was stuffing myself. I have never deprived myself of eating anything I really wanted. I was just now eating a lot less of it.

3. In order not to feed the cancer cells or have a glucose problem triggered by steroids, I cut down on sugar. I never completely eliminated it and occasionally indulged in a sliver of dessert, but I do think that this reduction had a lot to do with reducing cravings to graze and overeat.

4. There is solid scientific evidence from research with mice that the same caloric intake of a control group who ate whenever they wanted compared to the experimental group of mice with restricted intake of within an 8-hour time window within a 24-hour period, i.e., fasting for 16 hours, resulted in about one third more weight loss for the same caloric intake. For me that has translated into the kitchen closing by 7pm and giving myself at least 12 hours rest from eating. For a chemo patient, I think this has an extra benefit because chemo destroys many of your digestive enzymes, so giving what is left a digestive rest seemed intuitively a good idea.

5. Another piece of intuitive wisdom is whether to drink water with meals. I had a lifelong habit of drinking at least one glass of water with meals. But I then learned that gastric bypass patients are forbidden to drink water with meals (same goes for any other drink). This is because it distends the stomach and dilutes the digestive enzymes, and this prevents them from doing their job in a timely fashion. Thus, prevailing wisdom is to drink the water an hour before or following a meal. If you must drink something, then try

sipping on a little water at room temperature laced with lemon, thus alkalizing the water. This advice has been hard for me to follow, but since chemotherapy patients like myself often suffer from heartburn and indigestion after eating, I can tell you that this improved things considerably.

6. I learned that softer foods were much kinder to my digestive system, and if they were not soft to begin with, then chewing more and slowly was a good idea. I had always wolfed down my food, the fastest eater in any group. This was a throwback to boarding school days as a teenager, where there was peer pressure to eat fast. The only way that your table of peers could go up for second helpings was when the whole table was finished. I am resolved, although it is difficult, to sustain this new fledgling habit.

7. I learned to finish my food if I felt full, and instead of being a member of the clean plate club, I gave away or threw out food I did not like or did not need to eat to feel satisfied. No longer was I chained to my childhood: "Remember the starving children in India."

Throughout my chemotherapy journey, I was learning to listen to my body and what it needed. By doing so, I was aiding in my own healing and creating what I intend to be lifelong habits. I now know the real meaning of eating to live and not living to eat.

LAST CHEMO TREATMENT
June 10th, 2014

No palpable tumors upon physical examination and absolutely all blood work within normal levels, including glucose, therefore no diabetes in sight. My efforts in reducing sugar have paid off, despite the glucose-elevating nature of steroids. I consider this a big achievement, especially with well-meaning friends repeatedly plying me with desserts, thinking I need fattening up. It is so difficult to explain that I am trying to avoid permanent neuropathy, diabetes, and potential amputation. Since I do not have 12 days of antibiotics to contend with, and anti-nausea meds will be increased, my oncologist thinks I could have an easier time of it this round. I certainly hope so. I brought up the topic of the customary five years of hormone meds that cancer patients usually take after treatment. The side effects of these hormones is horrendous; certain weight gain, osteoporosis, hair thinning, interference with high blood pressure pills (which I take), increased risk of heart attack and stroke, depression, bone aches. The list goes on. Dr Bardia reassured me that these hormones were not mandatory and wisely deferred discussing in depth the pros and cons to a later date. I am going to research alternatives in natural medicine. While I believe that healthy food choices such as cruciforous vegetables are helpful, I do not believe one can eat them in sufficient quantities to make a significant difference, because if that was the case I would have never contracted cancer in the first place. So the jury is still out on any natural avenues for treatment going forward.

My usual infusion nurse, Barbara, had a well-deserved vacation day, and today I got George, who was a hoot! He and Linda, who are both hyperactive extroverts, played off each other. All I had to do was lie back on my bed like a princess and enjoy the show. I just roared with laughter. The two of them were hysterical and they really wound each other up and got each other going. Who knew that my final infusion day could be fun! What a miracle!

It certainly helps my morale to have Jon around this time during chemotherapy to help with dinner and relieve my anxiety about business issues. He bought me a batch of his homemade rye crackers and a "Prayer Bear," which truly touched me. We are eating down my well-stocked freezer for dinners and I served a favorite of his, a bison tomato sauce served over angel hair pasta with a salad. Since I can be rather dopey around a hot stove after infusions, he takes over cooking when he arrives home. It is such a treat to have a man cook for me. Never had that in my entire life. We enjoy talking about how to cook food and favorite recipes. What a pleasure it will be to cook for him when I am well again.

LOOKING FORWARD
June 13th, 2014

It is three days post my final chemotherapy infusion and, despite it pouring with rain and needing to take anti-nausea meds before I eat, I find myself looking forward for the first time during this entire year. It has suddenly occurred to me that in a few weeks I will be able to taste my food properly and eat again some foods that I have had to avoid for being too bitter. Then, just think, I am going to be able to stride along in the open air instead of wobbling dizzily across a room in my house, banging into walls. And instead of watching the golfers go past my window, I will be joining them with joyous, careless abandonment! And my hair, eyebrows and lashes will start to grow again—what a miracle that will be! The neuropathy in my hands and legs will gradually abate. And the infection in my eyes will go away and, like all the other infected areas of my body, will return to normal. And little by little my brain will be sharp again.

I have lost sight of what it means to feel well, but when I get there it is going to taste so sweet!

I WANT A HAPPY LIFE AND TO CONTROL MY OWN FATE
June 14th, 2014

Somebody said on a TV program tonight that all they wanted was a happy life and to control their own fate. It sounds so ridiculously simple, doesn't it? But the sad reality is I haven't been happy these last few years, and my life certainly hasn't been under my control. I would never have chosen what I have now as my fate. When you come to think of it, so many of us have a life that is not to our choosing. It has always been somewhat mysterious to me, the fine balance between being at peace with what is now, and never giving up hope that you have the power to effect a better future for yourself or for others. I was talking to my friend Sandy this weekend about people who have hit rock bottom in their lives, in unimaginable ways, yet somehow have found the strength to pull themselves up from the sewers to develop happy and productive lives. They have faced far worse challenges than mine, and I am awed by their stories of recovering from drugs, parental abuse and more. Or those people who weighed over 400 pounds and now run several miles a day; they make my weight challenges seem trivial. Yet for each of us, as we face our own unique hurdles, our personal pain is very real.

It was Father's Day yesterday and someone on Facebook posted how they hated normal, happy families. I thought of when my life was happy and normal. It seems such a long time ago. I had a husband who loved me, a thriving business, no health challenges and we lived a very blessed life. Then it all changed. My husband got sick and died, my business fell apart, and my health fell off a cliff. I just want normal back again. I want to feel the wind in my hair as I walk along marveling at nature, I want to hold the hand of a man who loves me, and I want to see my business thrive again.

MY GARDEN
June 16th, 2014

My garden has always been a great source of joy to me. When I moved to Pinehills in 2005, I bought a house that faces east in the morning and catches the setting sun in the evening. In other words, an ideal plant-growing environment, and one that I never had before in my life from my prior north-facing gardens. I had decided to create an English perennials garden, which is a riot of color, but unruly to most American eyes. After some trial and error, I managed to fill it with as many different perennials, flowering shrubs, and colorful vines as would withstand the harsh northeast winters. Some favorite flowers just didn't make it, but most thrived due to the careful soil amendment that I did before starting the garden. Please know that my garden is tiny compared to a regular house, but I can guarantee you that I have more in it! No room for weeds to grow as every inch is covered! I worked over the years to make sure that there was always something in bloom, and augmented the color with some bright perennials in pots. Herman used to love my garden, and while he did not have a green thumb, he enjoyed it when I took him on the garden tour to identify flowers and show him what was in bloom next. He also adored it when I picked fresh flowers to put beside his favorite recliner chair when he lay so ill. Herman was proud of my garden and was never loathe to boast, to anyone who would listen, that I had the best garden in the entire community!

It probably would not surprise you to hear that after his death, I hardly went out in my garden. All I could remember was his walking up and down the garden, a safe place where he was allowed to walk without getting lost. Of course, I did the minimum upkeep, but my garden, like other areas of my life, fell silent, waiting for me to return to it.

This year, I decided that if I was to languish inside, that I might as well give myself a riot of annual color to look out on by my kitchen door sliders and out on my deck. Coupled with the enthusiastic support from Rosemarie, my new gardener, we planted pots and filled in some bare spots with something different. And at sunset I began to wander in my garden again, deadheading as I did with my slow chemo shuffle. But the garden made me smile and I replaced the white wicker deck furniture I had bought especially to please Herman, with another outdoors furniture set with cleaner and simpler lines.

Now I do my garden tours with any visitor to the house, sharing my joy with them. I particularly get pleasure showing Jon how my garden is growing. He is actually very knowledgeable about gardening, but as I show him what is coming and going in bloom on his visits, it has echoes of former and sweeter times. My garden is making me smile again and it is healing.

TURNING THE CORNER AT LAST
June 17th, 2014

My last chemotherapy infusion was June 10th, and I can now feel that the beast is slowly receding from burning its way through my system.

Slowly, ever so slowly, I can feel myself rounding that corner at last. There was a point where I could never envisage this day actually coming.

If you haven't already gathered, I can tell you now that the last five months have been indescribably hard. Wracked with insomnia, a stomach in knots, there was more than one night where the tears trickled down my face and I thought that going to Heaven would be easier. As I wobbled across the room, bumping into walls and clutching furniture for balance, I wondered if I would ever walk proud and tall again. I looked into the mirror at the bald apparition with thinning brows and no lashes and despaired whether I would see that beautiful woman once more. Every part of my body, including my lady parts, due to chemo thinning the skin, still hurts to touch. I toyed with my food, it burned going down, tried to tempt my appetite, and ate enough to satisfy my oncologist. I wondered if food would ever taste good. Would I regain my enthusiasm for cooking? My eyes needed bathing three times a day. I drooled and my nose just constantly dripped. And my brain became addled. I could not read or even watch television as it was too much effort. I could not remember anything from one moment to the next. I felt like a very old person. Of course, I am not recovered yet, but at least I can see that it will change, God willing, and chemotherapy and everything that it entails will never be part of my life again.

I tell you this to be candid and not whitewash chemotherapy. It is brutal. As you know, I have fought for my sanity and my otherwise characteristic optimistic outlook on life. Every time I would have the dark thoughts, I would then turn my mind to the miracles and blessings in my life, of which there are many.

My surgery is in three weeks time. Another chapter in my journey coming up.

COURAGE

Courage is not noisy or flamboyant.
It does not shout to the world "Look at me!"
Rather, courage is taking one more step, when there are no more steps to
give.
And then one more, again and again.
Quietly without fanfare.

THE BIRTHDAY PARTY
June 24th, 2014

My birthday (June 25th) coincided with being two weeks past my last infusion. Like any chemotherapy patient who staggers over the finish line, I felt that my life without chemo was surely worth celebrating. My friends agreed. Two of my angels, Rosemarie and Maureen, organized a potluck dinner with my friends from far and wide, those who had supported me in my journey to date. About 40 people showed up at Rosemarie and Rick's beautiful home and garden. Rosemarie appreciated the exquisite importance of this milestone, having walked in my shoes a number of years ago.

It was an evening that I will never forget for my entire life. It was just an oasis of love and joy in what has been such a desert of pain. It was quite overwhelming to have so many people in solidarity and expressing their caring and love for me in one room at the same time.

Before I cut the cake, I made a speech from the heart. I confessed that all my life I had not felt very lovable, although I had tried to live a purposeful life and contribute to my fellow man by healing others and educating them so that they could have happier and healthy lives. But when Herman said when he was sick with brain cancer, and that I ought to try hard to keep him alive, because when he was gone there would be no one left who loved me, it had sent an icy chill down my spine. Who indeed? I changed my will and instructed there be no funeral (after all, there would be no one wanting to attend) and just to bury me next to Herman and someone could say a few simple prayers by my grave side. When I first got news of my illness, I characteristically assured a few friends that I would be just fine. All I needed to do was cook and freeze meals and stock up on every basic grocery supply I could anticipate needing. But those people who stood before me at my party all knew better than I. They insisted on helping me. They drove me to my infusions and doctor appointments, they gave me practical advice, they ran my errands, they gave me thoughtful gifts. They fed me when my face was practically falling in my plate, and listened endlessly when I thought I could never get up and face the chemo beast again. The miracle is that I was learning to receive love, and let others take care of me. Now I was being filled up with the caring and love of others.

Lesson learned: I am surrounded by love and just never realized it.

MY BUSINESS
June 27th, 2014

I have not written much about my business, except to allude to some financial mismanagement by my former CFO, and that Jon would come in regularly to help me turn it around. I had been feeling very discouraged and incredibly stupid for not having realized what my CFO had been doing. The fact that it took the majority of my life savings to prop up the company just compounded the misery, but it was not always that way. Let me tell you how it all began.

In the mid 1990s I had just met Herman, my late husband. I knew I wanted to design my life so that I did not have to jump on a plane to see clients. I wanted to build a company again and not have the life of a management consultant. I wanted it to be something that contributed to people's health, but the what and the how eluded me.

As it so happened, I had suffered from brutal headaches for over ten years and had taken some rather high test medication to banish the headaches and get going each day. The cause of the headaches was mysterious. I had trailed around to 18 different doctors who had given me 18 entirely different diagnoses. I was discouraged and frustrated, even more so when doctor #18 told me I was depressed and wanted to give me Prozac. I could be forgiven for being depressed, but far from it; I was madly in love and happier than I had been for years. But it was my late husband Herman who solved the problem by noticing that when we were at the beach or mountains, I woke up clear-headed and did not need any medication. He told me that I was allergic to my beautiful antique house. He wondered that I had environmental allergies, which was something he had seen occur in patients at his own clinical psychology practice. I skeptically trundled off to an allergist, doctor #19, who confirmed what my husband suspected, that I was allergic to everything that moved, including my beloved Siamese cats.

So with characteristic zeal, I researched online as to what to do to create an allergy-free home for myself. I wanted to keep my cats and I did not want to be taking allergy meds for the rest of my life. In the process, I discovered many things I could do that did not cost any money, just a bit of elbow grease. There were products I tried out whose curative effects were blatantly misdescribed, and a few others that really made a difference. My "get well to-do" check list grew to some 70 items long. It was about halfway down the list that I realized I was magically cured. By this time we had moved house, and the joy I felt when I realized that I was now waking up clear-headed and no longer needed medication was indescribable.

When I saw my clients suffering from sinus headaches or allergies, I could not resist spreading the good news about my discoveries. It was my clients who told me that I should start a business around my newly found expertise. It was the early days of the Internet, and I could see the possibilities of reaching a large audience through this new medium. By 1998 I was designing the first AllergyBuyersClub.com website. The goal of the company was to educate people about the pluses and minuses of the products they were buying. My own experience had told me there were no perfect products. I made a presentation to the MIT Enterprise Forum in 1998 and was laughed out of court. Only one member of the audience, a man who became my lawyer, encouraged me to continue. In 1999 a firm of angel investors agreed to raise $1 million and represent me for a percentage of the shares of my company. This is when I discovered what "Vulture Capital" is all about. Every time we met, after I thought the deal was concluded, they just wanted a little bit more, and then just a bit more after that. After a deal was concluded, all signed, they suddenly reversed themselves, saying that they did not think I would make a very good CEO, and they did not believe in my basic concept. You could not possibly tell the truth about products and then actually sell them. For their trouble in tearing up the contract they took 10% of my stock. I paid them out several years later. I loathed and despised them.

But I was left penniless. Credit card and mortgage debt up to my eyeballs. A huge legal bill to pay off, and the company's monthly gross sales were only $14,000, barely enough to pay my one assistant and other expenses. I set about cracking the secrets of search engine optimization, and I believed I was making progress. The only problem is I was broke and my husband Herman, who was crippled by alimony, did not have a dime to spare. As luck would have it, my ex-husband Eric, with whom I was on cordial, if not distant terms, commissioned me to build him a website that would get him to the top of the Google search engines. My business plan told me in six months I could get to break-even, and this money could just tide me through. Now I was working 16-hour days, seven days a week, and my husband Herman was very unhappy and threatened to throw my computer in the trash. Understandably, he wanted his wife back. By October 2000 we were grossing $100,000 a month. We were on a roll, with an enviable growth rate. For the next few years we could do nothing wrong, and I felt vindicated.

But by about 2008, a recession was in full bloom, competitors were nipping at our heels left and right, and margins had shrunk. Suddenly it was not so easy anymore, so I did the unthinkable and had my first layoff, and thought I had balanced our budget. By 2011, when my husband was diagnosed with brain cancer, I actually thought the company was in good shape. Little did I know that my CFO had begun to feed me false financials. There was a nightmare brewing under my nose and I was clueless. I liked and trusted this man; it never occurred to me that he could be lying to me. I never saw it coming. It was Jon who alerted me to the fact that there could be financial irregularities going on in my company. He had to voice his suspicions several times and quite vigorously before I could bring myself to bring in auditors, which then precipitated a confession from my CFO. I was devastated, as what had happened was unthinkable.

Jon pulled me back from the brink of disaster and gave me the courage to fight for the survival of my company and the jobs of my employees. The damage was in seven figures, and it took the majority of my retirement nest egg to underwrite the company. For many months, the news got worse and worse as layer after layer of mismanagement and malfeasance was revealed. It seemed unending and was incredibly stressful, since I no longer had enough money to retire on comfortably. My whole lifestyle and my happiness in living in my community was in jeopardy. After everything I had gone through with Herman and his brain cancer, this seemed beyond unfair, and could have crushed me if Jon had not intervened and lent his support.

In 2013 I got an unsolicited offer to buy the company from a public company whom I had known for years and who would have been a good strategic fit, and certainly had deeper pockets than I. I felt if I sold the company, it would give it better financing, which it sorely needed, and I could have a bigger and more interesting role to play. Jon and I explored this option for five months till it unexpectedly fell apart through no fault of our own. It was at that point we turned to Plan B, a turnaround by our bootstraps, which was again far more challenging than either of us realized. I have a very loyal and devoted staff, but they were used to doing things a certain way, and despite the fact that the old ways were clearly not working, they were very reluctant to change. If that wasn't difficult enough, I then got word of my cancer, and since then Jon has been coming every couple of weeks for a few days at a time to spearhead turning around the company. I have been learning from him how to be a better CEO. We do not agree all the time, and have had some very spirited debates. But I have been learning and growing. Some of my staff have been growing too. Others in senior key positions think they are working hard, but are fighting Jon tooth and nail about changing anything they do. The company is not profitable yet, although showing some glimmering signs of revival. How I long to be well and more active again in my work. I just refuse to give up.

PRACTICAL ADVICE FOR SURVIVING CHEMOTHERAPY
June 28th, 2014

Surviving chemotherapy requires fortitude, self advocacy and creativity. I am passing on some learnings in the hopes that somebody at a later date will find something that is useful to them. I also hope that my candor will not be offensive, but you need to understand that the side effects of chemotherapy do not constitute a pretty picture. Each person will encounter a different collection of side effects, but I managed to get acquainted with a good number of them.

BreastCancer.org is a website that lists most of the possible side effects of breast cancer, if you are a glutton for punishment.

Swallowing Problems

On the morning I woke up from my first infusion, I found I could not swallow. Food felt like razor blades going down my throat, and then landed in my stomach like a cannon ball. I was in agony and had no idea what was going on. It was actually a bit terrifying, since I wondered how was I going to survive chemotherapy if I could not even get food down. I had hardly begun the 5-month chemo marathon and I was in deep trouble. Luckily, a nurse from MGH made a follow-up call a couple of days later and told me to get on Prilosec immediately, otherwise I would damage my esophagus. I also got a little well-deserved lecture on how I should have called the hospital earlier and told them about this.

Belching

I belched far more than usual during chemotherapy, and was glad to be living alone so I could do it in peace. The frequency was very anti-social and highly embarrassing. It was far worse during the Taxotere round but it was still very prevalent during my A/C round. Taking daily Prilosec helped, as did taking an additional Prilosec occasionally before an evening meal. Of course, I stopped drinking carbonated beverages immediately and ate softer, easier to digest foods. I soon learned to avoid harder to digest foods, which for me included meat, and I upped my fish intake. The best thing I did to help my digestion was to stop drinking water with meals and only drink 30-45 minutes before or after eating. I got this tip from my massage therapist, Steve, who told me that gastric bypass patients are not allowed to drink water with meals, as it extends and bloats their stomachs as well as slows down the digestive process. I then did some further Internet research on the topic and verified his advice. Apparently, drinking water will dilute the gastric juices needed for digestion and then the food is more likely to be turned to fat. I stopped drinking water with meals and noticed an immediate reduction in belching. It was one of the best things I did to help myself and I wish I had known sooner.

Nausea

Zofran was the only drug that had any chance of keeping nausea at bay, and my stomach felt queasy for five months. It never felt like anything approaching normal, and I had to take more doses of anti-nausea meds than is usual, and yes, despite the meds, I threw up a few times. But I learned pretty darn quickly which foods were likely to set me off, and from then on avoided them like the plague. All I can say is don't be shy about taking your anti-nausea meds. They are there for a reason.

Tastebuds

My tastebuds radically changed from day one, although I never got a metallic taste in my mouth or completely lost my sense of taste.

However, most food did not taste really good and much tasted down-right awful. Most often than not, some food tasted too sour, and to my embarrassment at some social occasions, I had to push it away in disgust. It was not always predictable, but I learned quickly enough to avoid some things, like many salad dressings.

Softer foods like eggs, mashed potatoes and meat sauces (sweetened with Truvia), or even chili sat well with me. Homemade soups with no salt were a blessing. Unfortunately, spicier foods and wine came off the list immediately. Your tastebuds do regenerate after chemotherapy quite quickly, just a number of weeks. Again, there was no obvious reason behind the speed or order in which foods tasted good again. At the beginning, I craved sweet things like I had never done before in my life. However, I realized I was on a slippery slope and eliminated almost all sugar from my diet before I escalated out of control.

Constipation

Your doctors will warn you that the anti-nausea meds are constipating and to keep ahead of the game with Senna and Colace. All I can say is being proactive was excellent advice. Although I ate lots of fruit, veg-etables, and beans, which would be sufficient in normal times to keep my system moving, the anti-nausea meds, whether Zofran or Com-pazine, brought my system to a grinding halt. Sometimes it is hard to realize just how strong these medicines really are and the side effects are not in our imagination. This one, I can assure you, is very much for real.

Hemorrhoids

It can be shocking to the uninitiated to see bloody stools and blood in the toilet bowl. When I expressed concern to my oncologist he said he wasn't concerned about the blood indicating cancer is pres-ent since I was already on chemo. This continued for several months and the best explanation I got from a breast cancer survivor was that it was due to thinning skin, which happens all over including inside your body.

Vulva Pain

Perhaps one of the worst pains of all, also due to thinning skin, was in my vulva area. Every time I urinated, the outside vulva area would burn. In the end, I took two consecutive doses of antibiotics, which lessened the urgency but not the exterior pain. This pain was constant for several months and was extraordinarily debilitating. The best thing I was able to do for myself was apply apple cider vinegar and cold water compresses through the night, and often during the day. Coconut oil was also soothing.

Skin Care

Almost overnight my skin, which had always been excellent, dried up and felt like sandpaper, and my face suddenly showed a lot of wrinkles. I was horrified. My arms and legs felt rough to the touch. I experimented with a number of supposedly deep hydrating skin creams, but nothing was really doing the job.

In the end, I turned to organic coconut oil, which I used liberally all over my body, including my face, and as I mentioned earlier, including my genital region. I also put it on my flaky, dry, bald scalp. I managed to eliminate the encrusted, flaky skin on my scalp by soaking my head in coconut oil for a couple of hours and then very gently with a tissue exfoliating several layers of dry, flaky skin. It was quite a production. Then at night I put a deep moisturizer on my head while I was still bald. The coconut oil, a suggestion from my friend Sandy, was simply amazing and the skin on my arms and legs felt incredibly soft and smooth. What a miraculous find and one that was kind to my skin and to my pocket book.

Touch Sensitivity

I did not get bone ache, but my body became very sensitive to touch and my massage therapist had to go very lightly on me compared to our usual deep tissue massages before chemotherapy. This is probably in part due to the thinning skin everywhere on my body. My face really hurt to touch, which was odd and unpleasant. I didn't want to be touched and hugging my friends was very perfunctory. This does abate over time, and I love the comfort of human touch, but light stroking was far more agreeable.

Neuropathy

I had neuropathy in my hands and feet, which started almost immediately in the Taxotere rounds. When I first experienced it, it felt like my finger tips had been placed on a burning stove. It was horrendous. Shortly afterwards my feet followed suit and I could not walk across the floor in my stockinged feet because they hurt so much and my ankles ballooned out. The best thing for my feet was massage, and with the change to the A/C round my neuropathy symptoms lessened, but not before I had dropped a number of plates and glasses on the kitchen floor and had a number of minor accidents. Neuropathy does not disappear overnight. As we speak it is improving, but I am told symptoms can linger for a year or so, and for some people it never leaves.

Eye Irritation

Yet again, my friend Sandy came to the rescue when I complained of constantly itching eyes and accumulation of crusty stuff all around my eyes. She had me bathe my eyes with baby soap on a wash cloth, rinse, and just gently wipe away the debris that stuck to my few eyelashes. I had to do this three times a day, in addition to using eye drops. In the end, I abandoned eye makeup until my eyes recovered. My eyes were not a pretty sight.

Dripping Nose and Drooling

There's nothing like a constantly dripping nose (I had no nasal hair) and drooling out of the right side of my mouth to make one feel like I was joining the ranks of the senile. I was constantly dabbing with a tissue. Thankfully this went away pretty fast, so it was no longer a source of public embarrassment.

Nosebleeds

I have never suffered from nosebleeds my entire life, but as soon as I started the first rounds of chemotherapy my nose could not stop bleeding, and I was constantly dabbing at my bloody nose. For someone who never had nosebleeds before, it was a bit disconcerting. I did try extra humidification in my bedroom and nasal sprays, but nothing seemed to really help. It was something that happened during the three months of Taxotere rounds but not in the later A/C rounds.

Mouth Sores

I was lucky enough to avoid the worst of mouth sores, although early on I did rinse my mouth several times a day with a combination of salt and baking soda. Your physician will prescribe a medicine called "miracle wash" if your mouth gets really sore. I was constantly rinsing my mouth to free food debris since I had less saliva around to do the job naturally. I also flossed my teeth twice a day to make sure that bacteria did not accumulate in my mouth. I am sure that helped.

Dental Care

I went to the dentist just before I started chemotherapy for a routine cleaning. It is not recommended that you have dental care during chemo for fear of bleeding and infection. I flossed my teeth twice a day during my chemo and my at-home dental care was quite frankly, never more conscientious.

Insomnia

I was very sensitive to the steroids, which gave me terrible insomnia for days upon end until the effects wore off. I was lucky if I got much more than three hours sleep each night. I listened to relaxation music via Pandora to help the hours pass, and to assist me in drifting back to sleep. That was probably the best thing I did for myself. I was already taking melatonin before chemo started. My oncologist gave me Ativan. Nothing worked well and my oncologist had me see a specialist at MGH to prescribe heavier duty medication for a very short while, as I was becoming desperate for a good night's sleep. Getting a good night's sleep is very important, as the fatigue from endless insomnia will not help your fight against cancer. I can only suggest that you do not suffer in silence and work with your oncologist immediately to improve your sleep. It is a very common side effect and doctors are used to working with patients to manage it. My sleep was disturbed during my entire five months of chemo, but take heart, it does finally return to normal. And when it did, I rejoiced!

Fatigue

Fatigue is a side effect of the chemo meds and the disturbance in sleep, and increases in intensity during the chemo treatment. During the last month of chemotherapy, I only went into work a couple of days and became the queen of extensive naps. This fatigue was very frustrating to me, as I was used to being such a high energy person. To find myself huffing and puffing just walking across the room or feeling exhausted after just a few minutes of doing some trivial household chore was quite astonishing and very unnerving. It took me a long time to come to terms with this lack of energy, because I truly fought to keep my life normal for as long as possible. My advice is that there is no shame in pacing yourself. I learned to spread out my chores and go easy on myself and to stop worrying about it. Everyone told me the fatigue passes, and I will get back up to full speed when all my treatment is over. As the chemo recedes, it is absolutely true that you get stronger each day. Remember that.

Driving

My reaction times with driving really deteriorated during the Taxotere rounds. What driving I did was in the slow lane, and friends drove me to medical appointments in Boston, where my reaction times would not have been fast enough. There were times when I knew I was lucky to get home safely, so I restricted my driving, and would drive early in the day before I became too tired. Luckily during the A/C round I found my driving improving, and it was only fatigue that kept me from driving longer distances.

Unfortunately, I still had to keep mopping my streaming eyes during my driving, since my vision blurred very easily.

Static Hypotension and Balance

I have always had excellent balance and was aghast to discover, after I had been sitting or lying down for a while, how dizzy I would feel when I stood up. I had to clutch onto something to avoid falling over. It is a known side effect of Taxotere, which was included in my first four rounds of chemo. This dizziness did not dissipate quickly and I had to be very careful. When I got home from a lengthy car ride, I had to breathe and hold onto the car for support. Other times, like when getting out of bed to go to the bathroom, I would bang into walls. Hydration is one of the known remedies. I wished I could have hydrated more, but the pain and inconvenience from extra bathroom trips was one I wanted to avoid at all costs. All I can say is be very careful, and if you experience fainting, let your oncologist know immediately.

Chemo Brain

This is a very real phenomenon, especially in the Taxotere rounds. It was really quite frightening to witness my brain turning to non-focused mush. I could not concentrate on anything properly, whether it was work issues or even reading or TV. And my short-term memory all but evaporated. I could only listen to music, and strangely enough found I could write the first draft of this book, because the words came pouring out without involving concentration. During the A/C rounds my brain really improved but to remember names, like the flowers in my garden, I had to devise word association tricks for myself. When I gave what appeared to be an impromptu speech at my birthday party, I had to rehearse more than usual, but did manage it without notes. Every day I played bridge on my computer, both for enjoyment and to sharpen my memory. I am told that the residual effects of chemo brain can last months, if not years. Personally, I think that you do have to work a bit at helping those brain cells regenerate. At the moment, I am a work in progress.

Hair Loss

I have written elsewhere about the mental anguish that occurs when you lose your hair. It will always remain for me one of the most painful parts of having cancer, because I had to look at myself in the mirror, and it was an ugly reminder of reality. I never got to thinking "bald but beautiful."

My hair was cut very short about three weeks into the Taxotere round, as it was coming out in handfuls. During the A/C rounds I gradually became completely bald. I have written above how I used coconut oil to moisturize and exfoliate the dead, flaking skin from my scalp. When I was by myself at home, I just walked around with a bald head. I even drove the car while bald. A wig was part of my public face even though, especially during summer, a wig is not exactly comfortable, and I was prone to perspiration. At times I would have loved to rip it off my head. As chemotherapy ended, I gathered enough steam to focus on doing what I could to promote the growth of healthy hair again, and took heed of the advice of a hair specialist that perms and curling tongs should not be in my future. I am not a fan of grey hair, so I will color it again. To me grey hair is ageing. Given that I have had a lifelong aversion to short hair, wigs will be part of my life for some time to come, probably the better part of two years given the usual length of my hair.

Eyebrows and Eyelashes

I lost 75% of my eyebrows and lashes by the end of five months of chemotherapy, despite using lash and eyebrow building products. Quite frankly, towards the end of my 5-month chemo journey, it was the least of my worries. I also kept losing some lashes after the five months was over. Reluctantly, I became reconciled to my bald eyes and did not disguise it with eye makeup because of my eye irritation. I was told that, like my hair, it would all grow back. Right now I am still patiently waiting for my Brooke Shields bushy eyebrows to reappear.

Wigs

Wigs can be a blessing and the bane of your existence. Some people prefer soft cotton scarfs or turbans. I was not one of the latter because I did not want to look like a chemotherapy patient. Every time I put on my wig I could see that the beautiful woman was not completely lost, and that gave me hope for the future. Synthetic wigs are lighter and more comfortable than human hair, and monofilament wigs are the most realistic looking at the hair line. I had a selection of three in the end. I found Racquel Welsh to be a good brand, but there are surely others. My problem was the paucity of wigs in a large size. I did get advice for fitting, wig care, and how to wear a wig from a wig store. Something I very highly recommend and wish I had done sooner. Since I had to start wearing a wig within three weeks of starting chemo, I advise putting this very high on your action item list. I did enjoy not having hairdressing bills and the "just plop on the wig and go" in the mornings without hair styling. But when people tell you that wigs are hot and uncomfortable, they are right. My wig was my public face to the world. And the day I do not need to wear a wig anymore except for fun will be truly welcome.

Nails

I have regular manicures, and my manicurist was careful not to push back my cuticles and always has a bag of tools set aside just for me with my name on them. During the Taxotere chemo series my nails became very brittle and kept breaking, even though I keep them pretty short. They also turned a deep shade of ugly yellow, and threatened to lift off, but thankfully nail polish covered a multitude of sins. Miraculously, during the A/C round of chemo my nails started to grow again at their usual rate. It was very strange when the nail polish was removed to see the top half of my nails a deep shade of yellow and the lower half white again. It was a private thrill to see myself with nice nails again. Please note, I took both Biotin and Silica supplements during chemo to strengthen and grow my nails. My toenails were another matter. At the beginning of chemo I had a little toenail fungus, courtesy of my late husband. During chemo, the fungus spread and all my nails turned a deep shade of orangey yellow. My friends would talk about their pedicures while I hid my ugly toes inside my socks.

Weight

I have written at great length about my struggles with weight, which surely preceded chemotherapy. However, a significant number of people gain weight due to the steroids, lack of physical activity, and turning to comfort food. Some even develop diabetes. Others, of course, lose weight due to lack of appetite, fatigue and nausea. The goal is to stay as even as possible, and while my weight bounced around a bit, I did remain almost even. I logged what I ate and adjusted accordingly to eat within a healthy caloric range. I joined a private weight loss group on Facebook with people I knew, just to be conscious about what I ate. I worked hard to bring down my glucose levels. The Facebook group accepted that in the short term I had different goals. It worked well for me.

In the end, I had to be brutally frank with friends who were lovingly pushing desserts on me. This is what I said: "Cancer cells feed off sugar and I want to beat this thing. I already have neuropathy, so if you don't want me to have permanent neuropathy and diabetes and possible amputation, do not feed me sugar." Later on I said: "I am dieting. Obesity raises the incidence of reoccurrence of cancer. So if you don't want me to have a mastectomy or stage 4 terminal cancer, do not over feed me or give me sugar." That shut them up, but I had to say it multiple times to some dear friends whom I wanted to strangle.

You will gain water weight purely due to the steroids you are likely taking. I knew that I had water weight because my ankles puffed up, as did my face. My ankles were of most concern to me because of the neuropathy and getting blood flow to my feet. My massage therapist and my pilates instructor were helpful here. Sitting with my feet elevated also helped. The water weight was worst in the Taxotere round because I was taking twice the steroid dose. During the A/C round I negotiated with my oncologist for less Decadron doses because of its effect on my sleep.

MUSIC, A SOURCE OF CALM
June 27th, 2014

Mediation music, which I channelled through Pandora on the Internet, was my constant companion during Decadron induced insomnia. Instead of the chirpy Zumba music that I had been used to playing upon waking up each morning, I found a gentler genre of music far more soothing. When all semblance of concentration had disappeared, and I could not read or even watch television, then music was what was left. I cannot recommend it more strongly. I found listening to music very calming, as long as I stayed away from emotional vocals, when the tears would fall. When I play my Zumba music one day again in the mornings, I will know that I am better at last.

MY CATS, UNCONDITIONAL LOVE
June 28th, 2014

I have been a committed cat lover my entire life, and since I was introduced to Siamese cats over 40 years ago, I have been a fan of the breed. I have had several generations of Siamese cats and my current cats, HoneyBear and Truffles, have done a sterling duty in keeping me company throughout my chemotherapy. In fact, they love that I am home more often. They regard my bed at night as one big happy cat basket, and we all curl up together. Being able to reach out and stroke one of their little warm bodies at night when I had insomnia was immensely comforting.

Truffles is the male, an 8-year-old Applehead Bluepoint, and is very affectionate and needy. Anytime I wake up and go to the bathroom, he insists on accompanying me (I will spare you the details) and then rushes back onto the bed where he covers me with kisses and purrs so hard I think he will choke. I feel bad about waking up, since that is often his cue to harass HoneyBear and chase her off the bed. She is now 13 and just wants a quiet life, and desires nothing better than to just cuddle up to me. That clearly irritates him, and he is quite ruthless in vanquishing her from the bedroom. He has also found a new victim in Jon, who has never had a relationship with a cat before, and they have an after dinner ritual that involves Truffles jumping up onto his lap after Jon lays down his dinner napkin. If he thinks Jon is loitering over his food too long, he attempts a sneaky approach from the rear of the chair. Truffles is a talker and will chat happily back and forth with you for hours on end.

I have always been an animal lover, the more so because their affection is clearly unconditional, and I feel very privileged to be clearly loved by another species. Getting through this illness would have been that much harder without them as I have never felt completely alone. Animals are God's gift to man.

TRUFFLES AND HONEYBEAR

Truffles, cat, that gorgeous beast,
Looks at nighttime as his fancy feast
He proudly accompanies me to bed,
And grooms the fur on top my head,
In ecstasy, he loudly purrs,
And tells me we just have different furs.
HoneyBear slithers in close beside my ear,
Purring loudly, so I can hear.
Truffles then begins to frown,
He wants me for his very own,
He swats her with his big fat paw,
Right on her face and even jaw.
But soon we settle down to sleep,
Silence reigns, and not a peep.

Mercia Tapping

LOVE THY NEIGHBOR
June 29th, 2014

I have always considered myself to be a deeply spiritual person, who has tried to conduct life as a good person who contributes to others. However, I admit to not having reflected deeply on the Ten Commandments, and am not affiliated with any traditional religion. But Herman's death changed me. It showed me that, apart from your health, the most important thing in life is love. So without really realizing it, I set about bringing a little bit of love and joy into the lives of others on a daily basis. Just very small things and little surprises to my friends, as I shared my flowers or latest recipes. Sometimes it was saying something nice to a perfect stranger. It wasn't as if I had lived my life as a selfish person, far from it, but apart from my husband, I did not focus so much consciously on the lives of others and how to bring a smile to their faces. At some point during my chemotherapy, when others were going out of their way to bring me comfort and moments of joy, I finally got the true meaning of that commandment "Love Thy Neighbor," and it moved me to tears and I wept at its profound wisdom.

Lesson learned: Love thy neighbor as thyself. How often have we heard those words? But when you truly understand them, it touches you to the depths of your soul.

LOVE IS IN THE SMALL THINGS
July 1st, 2014

I wrote this a couple of years ago when I was grieving about the loss of my husband and what I enjoyed about being in a couple relationship. Note that it has nothing to do with sex, although physical touch is included. It is more about a man who is my best friend and delights in my company.

Love is in the small things and that is what I miss:

- Someone whose face lights up when I walk through the door.
- Someone who makes me giggle and laugh.
- Someone who yells out "great shot, honey," when I actually pull off a good one on the golf course.
- Someone who tells me how pretty I look when I get dressed up, or have been to the hairdresser.
- Someone who holds my hand when we go for a walk along the harbor or beach.
- Someone who actually cares how my day went.
- Someone who insists on doing the household errands together, just because they love my company and will help me with the heavy lifting.
- Someone who appreciates the effort I put into cooking dinner for us both, and enjoys our conversation over dinner.
- Someone to curl up with for a nap after an invigorating golf game.
- Someone who goes with me to big medical appointments, because they know deep down I am scared.
- Someone who roots for me in whatever I am up to next.
- Someone who allows me to be me, and does not want me to be anyone else.
- Someone who has got my back in a crisis or when the chips are down.
- Someone who can listen and stand firm if I wobble.
- Someone who tells all our friends that he is the luckiest man alive to have found me.

I missed these things in my life for over three years, and it is what I want in a future couple relationship. A girl can still dream, even at my age. No one is never too old to live happily ever after.

NOT SO FAST
July 4th, 2014

Naturally, with chemo behind me now for over three weeks, I harbored the fantasy that I would bounce back and all my side effects would magically disappear. Hmm, it doesn't work like that, although if I look back to a whole week ago, I can see some progress. At least my "female" problems and pain are abating after three excruciating months, my sleep pattern is back to normal, and my brain is perking up. I have enough of my brain back to be writing articles for my company, and that feels like such an accomplishment. And my fingernails are growing like a weed and the new nails are a delightful, healthy shade of white and pink. But I am still fatigued beyond imagination, and I quite regularly crash for a couple of hours in the afternoon. Other symptoms such as mouth sores, loss of eyebrows and lashes, and tearing eyes continue, which has surprised me, since I would have expected them to cease before now. But, oh joyous rapture, my tastebuds are returning bit by bit, and while there are some things still off my menu, I am starting to enjoy food again! However, I continue to make an abysmal dinner guest, as I am still a very picky eater, and gone are the days of wolfing down anything put in front of me!

I went for my prep and post-operative education and information at MGH a couple of days ago. It was very detailed, emotionally intense, and exhausting. The prep is relatively simple, but I flinched when I learned that the amount of breast tissue being removed was close to the size of two eggs, and when I saw the size of the drain that needs to be emptied three times daily from the lymph nodes under my arm (10-30 will be removed) for about two weeks, I felt distinctly nauseous. I am such a wuss! I will not be able to drive until the drain is out, but will be able to hunt and peck on my iPad and do some work from home after the initial pain subsides. And in order to avoid, or at any rate minimize, lifelong fluid retention in my left arm, I will have a plethora of daily exercises to follow. The doctors still swear that I will get full use of my left arm back to go golfing again, but it is clear that I will have to work at it. Thank goodness that I do pilates. The big day is Friday, July 11th, a week from now. If I get clear margins, then they will not have to repeat the procedure. After a modest time to heal, I will proceed to radiation. One step at a time.

POST SURGERY
July 14th, 2014

I had breast cancer surgery on Friday, July 11, and stayed overnight and came home Saturday, July 12th. Jon was with me every step of the way on the day of the surgery, and stayed with me from 5:30am till 8:00pm and was back by breakfast next day. What a blessing, as I truly needed his support, his calming influence, and the warmth and comfort of his hand. We both had several misty eye moments. Everything took much longer than anticipated, which was partly caused by the fact that even under ultrasound, the visible cancer had all but disappeared. I was very relieved that I was in the hands of such experienced doctors, since I surmised that nothing about my surgery was routine. I had made a declaration in January that it was my intention that all visible cancer would be gone by the end of chemotherapy, and that by doing so I would have the choice to avoid a full mastectomy. So that happened, even the mammogram technician remarked that, with such a lot of visible cancer on my initial pictures, a radical mastectomy was more usual. My sister was dumbfounded when I told her that the cancer was pretty much gone, because she remembered my resolve to disappear it, six months ago. Even so, 25% of my left breast has been removed, plus 28 lymph nodes. I am, of course, feeling like my chest has been involved in gang warfare, and I am creeping around rather gingerly. I am only taking Tylenol, having refused Vicodin, and have shuffled outside, walking around the block a couple of times. I had actually managed twice around the block and a whole 23 minutes by Sunday evening. I was very proud of myself. Of course, I am huffing and puffing, but trying to keep moving as much as possible and do normal chores. But as you might expect, I have very limited energy, and the visiting nurse said to expect fatigue even when the drain is removed. So meanwhile, the nap queen has full reign.

I always try to find a silver lining to everything and I can tell you that general anesthesia is one heck of a way to potentially lose weight. I have given up on my food log this week. Mother Nature is dictating light eating this week. I am certainly eating enough, no worries there, but no inclination to wolf down a whole lot of food. It would be nice if I broke the next decade in weight loss by the time the drain comes out. We shall see. So for now, back to resting.

A BIG DAY
July 23rd, 2014

Yesterday was a big day up at MGH, as I met with all the doctors who comprise my care team to discuss next steps. My breast wound is healing well, but if I want the drain out from under my arm where the lymph nodes were removed, I need to stop my diligent arm exercises until after it is out and deal with arm and shoulder stiffness later.

I also learned, from the surgeon and others, that I had given him "grey hairs" last week. My surgery was complex because of the unusually large amount of tissue removed, without it being the whole breast. It took longer than usual because of the extra care he took to put the breast back together, so it was aesthetically pleasing. Most people would have opted for a radical mastectomy (or be told they needed one). I am very thankful that I was in the hands of a top surgeon, since, as of this moment, I wouldn't even see the necessity for breast reconstruction. My oncologist was grinning from ear to ear, as chemo had clearly done its job, even better than I had thought, and he referred to radiology as "mopping up," and said I was now cancer free. He knows I am reluctant to go on the hormones scheduled for the end of this year, for 5-10 years duration, because of the side effects, but he's at least open to discussing a naturopathic hormone approach if I give him material to read on the matter. I am also due to go back on Herceptin antibody infusions every three weeks beginning late August, for nine months. I met a wonderful female radiologist, Dr Bernstein, with whom I totally fell in love. I need 33 sessions (six and a half weeks), a longer than usual treatment regimen, as it involves the lymph node area and very sensitive nerve endings. Treatment starts at the end of August at the earliest. She said she quite understood if I wanted radiation treatment to be carried out at a hospital nearer home, but I felt such a connection with this woman, I wanted to be her patient. It will be quite a daily trek of over 50 miles into Boston, but I think it is important to both like and have faith in your doctors.

You would think that with all this essentially good news that I would be elated, but in truth I arrived back home exhausted, and later in the evening, just profoundly sad and deflated. There was something in all the "happy" news I got yesterday that underscored the seriousness of my diagnosis, and the realization that I was going to be spending an inordinate amount of time in hospital this year. Despite my rebellion about being labeled a cancer patient, I was indeed one. As I mentioned, one of the options that I rejected was for radiation treatment to be closer to home. One of the hospitals is a perfectly lovely one where my husband was treated. Memories of my accompanying him there flooded back. With his brain cancer there was no cure, only a bit of extra precious time. He never got to be a «cancer survivor." I am one of the "lucky ones," where all the detectable cancer has been removed from my body.

Somebody the other day talked about "the good, the bad and the ugly" of having cancer. That struck a chord with me. Ultimately, when I actually die is not really my decision, but in the interim, whether I focus on the good and the miracles in my life IS my decision. But it is weak mental muscle that needs to be exercised since, when you have cancer, the inbuilt pull is to the bad and ugly—all the pain, discomfort, side effects and fatigue. Cancer gives plenty of fodder for the bad and the ugly. I am already weary of the fight, but I can only keep the faith that, somehow in this potpourri of emotions that I am experiencing, I will find my voice and have something to say that is of value to the rest of humanity.

THE GOOD, THE BAD AND THE UGLY
July 26th, 2014

I am beginning to discover, as I told you before, and as a friend of mine said recently, that the journey through cancer is a bumpy ride; anybody who thinks it is a straight line graph to recovery or that I "only had a lumpectomy," or some such nonsense, should walk in my shoes. I realize that I had what in many medical circles is called a "partial mastectomy" because of the amount of tissue and the 28 lymph node removal. A regular lumpectomy takes 1-2 hours operation; mine took over three hours, and my surgeon, who is brilliant, admitted that I gave him a challenge and a few grey hairs.

Although the drain is now out of my arm, it hurts like heck, especially in the evenings and during the night. I am supposed to use my arm very little in the next few days to head off fluid build-up under the wound. This includes a ban on driving, which I can quite understand, as every little bump in the road causes me to take a sharp intake of breath or a little yelp. So it is two weeks out and I am creeping around like I am over 90 years old and any small chore accomplished is a triumph. That is the Ugly.

I am sure it will sound strange to you that I continue to struggle with the label of "cancer patient" or "cancer survivor." The unsaid communication or subtext from my doctors is that others with my diagnosis do not respond to treatment as well as I have been doing. What they have actually communicated to me is how well I am doing, and that despite my cancer being stage 3, I am beating the beast. You would think I would be joyful and elated. Certainly my friends are near euphoric. No, there is a certain curious melancholy as I turn to face the next phase of my treatment and realize I will be living with the cancer cloud for a long time. That is the Bad.

But I keep telling myself to looking for the Good in all this, but it takes effort to do so when pain dominates my consciousness at times. Much to my delight, some of my chemotherapy side effects are receding, my digestion is not so cranky, and hallelujah, my tastebuds are returning! One of my big angels, Linda, took me out to lunch two days ago at a new restaurant, where instead of lemon making me screw up my face in disgust, which happened during chemo, I enjoyed an old favorite, Chicken Piccata. She also took me to a restaurant for dinner at a hut on the beach; the journey was a little rugged and I had to clutch myself to brace the bumps in the road, but the view of the ocean and the wonderful fresh fish dinner made the bumps more than worthwhile. The ocean is three miles from my house, and up till that moment, it could have been a million miles away. Just breathing in the ocean air and hearing the waves lap up against the shore was very soothing. And I have learned to rejoice in the small things. I peered under the magnifying mirror in the bathroom yesterday and saw little itty bitty eyelashes emerging, I was so thrilled I wanted to shout it from the rooftops! Maybe there will be an end to being the hairless wonder!

My friends are endlessly supportive and generous in taking me out to do necessary errands. Over the bridge table last night, my partner told me that there was nothing wrong with my brain! My chemo brain has been receding in a way that is a huge relief. That is also the Good. Now I go and Facetime with my sister Susan in England, whom I truly adore. She is one of the many blessings in my life.

Lesson learned: Keep searching for the good in life and you will find it, and then smile at your discovery.

ROSE
July 27th, 2014

One of my biggest angels supporting me is a woman in her mid-eighties named Rose. Although she has difficulty walking a good deal of the time, and cannot really drive at night anymore, she is one of those amazing people who does not wait for that call from me requesting help; she calls me up each day to check what she can do for me, and she does it with such good cheer and good grace. So she drives me around to do errands, and waits in the car as I shuffle around some stores, as I still have legs and one good arm. With much effort, she lifts my packages into the house and she also collects my mail every few days.

I have become exceptionally close to Rose. She is one of those few people with whom I can share all sides of "The Good, The Bad and The Ugly." I can talk freely about my health progress, or lack of it as the case may be, my business travails, and my dreams for a different kind of life when my cancer treatment has ceased.

Yesterday was a case in point, a day that could have been so lonely and frustrating, but Rose's company and actions made me smile. This may seem trivial to you, but we both went for manicures. It was a huge deal for me, as I had been wrapping cracked nails in tawdry looking paper tape to help keep them together. My nails had been lifting off with my chemotherapy and with one wrong move the nails threatened to rip off completely. My nails now look very strange. The bottom halves are pearly pink and white, the top halves are lifting off and are yellowed with ridges on them. Nail polish covers a multitude of sins, but my manicurist cut my nails ultra short and used silk patches to repair the cracked nails. The shorter nails will give me the courage to try a few additional household chores, and now the icky paper tape is gone!

After accomplishing some additional chores, Rose and I went to dinner at the Rye Tavern on our Pinehills campus. The Rye Tavern is one of those places that, in my opinion, is long on atmosphere but short on talent. They try incredibly hard to be creative and use herbs and different combinations, but have not learned the art of "less is more" and are very heavy handed with their herbs and spices, so they end up overpowering the food. Clearly you can see my tastebuds are returning! But the Rye Tavern is immensely popular, and does not need any cooking lessons or culinary hints from me. As Rose and I sat over our less than stellar dinner, we just enjoyed the conversation and she smiled at me and said, "This is almost back to normal!" That phrase stuck with me—"almost back to normal"—she must be seeing my progress perhaps more clearly than I. But I knew what she meant; at least I was emerging once more from the house to be sociable, instead of begging off with complaints of overwhelming fatigue. Perhaps there is light at the end of this tunnel and all I can say is "God bless Rose."

Lesson learned: Your true friends keep coming back to lift you up again when you need that help the most.

Rose

A friend can lend a hand
And listen with such clarity.
Sometimes more than you,
They can see who you were meant to be.

Mercia Tapping

INCHES AND NOT MILES
August 1st, 2014

One of the things that you learn, albeit reluctantly, in your cancer recovery is patience. This is especially hard to do for a Type A person like myself, so I am learning to celebrate progress in inches and not miles. Yesterday, as you know, I had a manicure that shortened and strengthened my nails. Armed with additional fingers, which now have been brought back into service, I decided it was time to embark on a new level of self care. I wanted to take a shower alone, put on a new lymph node bandage and zip up my SurgiVest, that charming garment that substitutes for a bra and keeps me rigidly in place, and I wanted to do it all unaided. Zippers have eluded me to date, and I was determined not to be forced into co-opting a bashful Jon into helping me next week, and bathing with baby wipes certainly just wasn't cutting it. MGH had shown me the "sure-fire way" to put on a new dressing with the aid of a big mirror, but it still required some as yet unachieved level of flexibility when my body was frozen in pain. But on Sunday morning, with a shower loudly calling out my name, I sallied forth. Perhaps sallying is too energetic a description, but it fitted my mood. I was determined to triumph! Needless to say, I was successful, but note this is 16 days post surgery.

Emboldened by my success, I dipped my newly minted fingers into coconut oil and slathered it all over my thirsty skin, which had been neglected since my surgery. You wouldn't think that putting coconut oil on my arms, legs and face should be such a big deal, and I feel a bit of an idiot with that admission, but it is the truth! As for cutting my toenails, well let's just say it required intense commitment to get the job done. And while I am about it, I can share with you my new creative way of getting my clean underwear out of the dryer. My body can reluctantly be coerced into taking things out from the front of the dryer, but rebels in pain to reaching out to collect things from the rear of the machine. So I said to myself, if people can learn to play the piano with their toes... Well I leave you to fill in the blanks!

I share this with you so that, if you are a caregiver, you will understand that people like me are not being lazy laggards; it is sometimes the small things that are overwhelming. And if you are, like me, making the cancer journey, then celebrate every little inch of your progress, for it is accomplished by inches and not miles!

I will be going out to lunch with friends in an hour and I will be feeling delightfully clean. Let's hear it for showers! The miracle of cleanliness!

Lesson learned: Go easy on yourself in your recovery journey and be patient. Learn to celebrate the seemingly small triumphs along the way, because they are not small at all.

THE BEST AND THE WORST OF TIMES
August 2nd, 2014

This last week Jon was in town continuing the battle alongside me to change the company culture and turn around the business so that it becomes profitable again. With scarcely two weeks of post surgery under my belt, I made the decision that, while I would avoid driving, I needed to go into the office before my employees imploded from the stress. Quite frankly, I would have preferred to stay at home one additional week, and it was not as if I was longing to return to work and face into all its problems, far from it. But the cries of distress from my employees had me decide that duty called.

I have always thought that Jon was brilliant, wise, and of course miraculously committed to helping me through my cancer journey, but I have truly struggled sometimes over the last seven months to understand his advice. On the one hand, I have had great faith in him, and I was doing my best to comprehend what he was saying. But a combination of chemo brain, physical pain and genuine puzzlement, or I daresay even resistance to his messages, has had me often frustrated and feeling totally inadequate, and certainly not up to the job. I felt I was never doing anything right in his eyes, and I could only see microscopic improvements in the business sales. So I could not even begin to say that my way was right. I knew it wasn't and change was imperative. Yet I lacked the drive to enable culture change in my company, and when Jon asked me to create a new vision for the future, I crabbily said to myself: "How the heck can I do that when I am so fatigued I get puffed from walking across the room? I cannot even sit or walk comfortably because of the infection in my female parts. I am managing some 20 plus chemo side effects, fighting for my life. I may have been superwoman in the past, but in cancer I have met my match, I cannot do it all."

So Jon valiantly sowed the seeds for culture change in my company in the first half of this year, with my staff kicking and screaming all the way. And while I could see we needed to change the way we did business, I had neither the clarity nor energy to make much happen. So we continued like many companies in trouble, to do what we knew how to do, but just work harder and a bit faster at it. Of course, we needed to change the way we conducted business in some very fundamental ways, but there was one big problem. The company's CEO was virtually absent, if not in body then in spirit for many months. If change is going to occur it needs to happen from the top down, and the top was missing in action. It was clear that my staff heard but disliked Jon's message, and longed for the day when I was recovered enough to be back at the helm, thinking of course that I would give them an easier ride, despite my warnings to the contrary.

The curious change that occurred over the next three days was that

Jon and I worked tirelessly together, shoulder to shoulder, seamlessly and without friction. For the first time, it seemed to me I was getting praise from him for my actions. And between us we were moving mountains and getting things done, as unpleasant as they surely were.

As Jon and I worked truly as partners in solving the company's problems, I had decided that instead of Jon tackling cooking at home in the evenings, that the weather was nice enough, and I had enough energy to take him out to dinner in Plymouth for various forms of outside dining. It was time to introduce him to summertime living in one of the loveliest parts of Massachusetts. I had been such a sad and sick sack for such a long time, and I wanted to show him and remind him that there was another side to me, one he hadn't seen in a very long while. There was a woman who could be a whole lot of fun and could laugh, and see the lighter side of life. So that is what we did in the evenings, we laughed as good friends do, sometimes till tears rolled down our faces.

One story that surely will go down in the annals of history, is on Wednesday night we were driving down the highway home, and Jon asked what our plans were for the evening. I had in mind that we needed to stop by CVS to see if there was any remedy to an itching scalp, as the first signs of life in my hair regrowth were occurring. I also remembered that Linda had made a dinner recommendation. We could stop off at a rather nondescript motel, which had a beautiful deck, mostly unpopulated by customers, right overlooking the ocean, and that had a light but very acceptable pub style menu, including huge lobster rolls. So this was the conversation and exchange between myself and Jon.

Jon: "What are we doing tonight?"

Mercia: "We have a couple of errands to run including CVS, but before we do that I suggest we stop off at a sleazy motel."

Then there was silence as Jon gripped the steering wheel, clearly struggling for a few seconds with what I had said. He reported to me later that he knew what I didn't mean, but did not know what I was actually trying to say. At last he voiced his confusion. Realizing what I had actually said and not communicated had me in tears, I was laughing so hard. Jon and I are just friends and he is so prim and proper. I just howled with laughter at my mistake, and before long he was chuckling too! We laughed about that one for the next 24 hours, and I remembered that one of our best common attributes was the ability to make each other laugh, and now we were doing it during one of the worst weeks of my business career.

I do know that we both felt the shift and change in our ability to work together, because when I expressed what I felt had been a seismic shift, he readily agreed, saying it had not been the usual push and pull between us.

EVERYDAY COURAGE
August 8th, 2014

Any cancer patient will tell you that you have to muster up every little piece of courage in your weary body in order to continue. Add the threat of bankruptcy or a fire sale for my company, and each and every day in my life is unbelievably hard to face. I search for little chinks of light, little signs of progress, but it takes a good deal of effort when I wake up into "I hate my life," and then I just pull myself together one more time, for another day.

I have been looking at my eyelashes growing at last in the mirror with some sense of incredulous wonderment. Yesterday, my 1.5-mile drive to collect my dry cleaning was a major triumph. I will surely be driving further afield soon. It is summertime, and every day I rejoice looking at my beautiful flowers in the garden and my view of the golf course. When friends drive me to the beach, it evokes all the good feelings embedded and sourced by memories of visits to the beach in my past. So there are good things, blessings and miracles every day, for which I am surely grateful. But when life throws crud into your face each day, you need to take a deep breath in order to rise up to the next challenge.

This last week at work, we have been faced with another extortionate demand from another patent troll. These are companies, as in my case, pursuing every e-commerce business on the web of a certain size, telling them they have violated umpteen patents, which are too expensive for small companies like ourselves to defend. So you are blackmailed into a settlement. The trolls squeeze as much out of you as they think you can afford. It is a dirty business because, for the most part, the patent infringements are not real, but incredibly loosely interpreted claims based on business processes. There is legislation in congress pending to stop this despicable business, but not before these blackmailers have hit my company up yet again. How I hate them, and our justice system for not protecting me.

My company faces numerous challenges on a daily basis. The stress has really started to get to me. A few nights ago I was up all night and dry heaved a couple of times. Even the most courageous can get overwhelmed by it all.

Jon arrives again next Monday. He is here in alternate weeks. In ten days time I get mapped out for radiation. I am not ready mentally for the next phase of treatment, yet I know it is coming.

Courage

Courage is taking steps when there are no more steps to take,
Yet moving forward is our only route to take.

Mercia Tapping

ESCAPE FROM REALITY
August 10th, 2014

Everyone whose life is as stressful as mine needs to find some escape from reality, even if just for a little while. It is a way to clear one's brain and to gather up enough energy to face the next round of treatment. What you choose to do is your choice, but I know unless you make an effort to take a break, you will sink without a trace. My timeout is weekends. This weekend was no exception.

My first stop this weekend was my manicurist. Besides having my nails look nice, my manicurist, Michelle, has brilliantly managed to save my chemo ravaged nails from completely falling off by cutting them very short and using silk patches to repair them. There is now enough of my nails attached to my fingers that this potential crisis has now passed, and I am less fumble fingered as a result. I can actually use my fingers without being fearful of ripping them off. So my nails made me smile.

I spent Saturday evening, as I often do, with my friend Sandy at her bed and breakfast. I took a couple of pounds of fresh, wild-caught cod with me, and Sandy cooked a healthy and comforting dinner for us and her husband, whom you may remember suffers from Alzheimer's. Conversations with Sandy are candid and soothing. There is no judgement in any of the advice she gives me, and she is the consummate caregiver. I get leftover breakfast treats from her freezer, which I have no trouble consuming, while I resist taking home her famous cranberry almond tart because I know I will eat it every night instead of watching my weight. Of course, I could not resist accepting just a tiny sliver of tart to have with my ginger peach tea after dinner. At Sandy's house, I feel relaxed enough to take off my wig and dine "au natural." As close girlfriends, we talk about everything, from our deepest hopes and fears, to how to take stains out of clothing, to where I can get my shirts laundered more cost effectively, while refusing Sandy's kind offer to iron my shirts. We swap plants from our gardens and natural remedies for all sorts of ailments. It is Sandy who turned me onto the wonders of coconut oil. Next weekend, we will most likely go to BJ's together, since I am running out of staples like toilet tissue and paper towels, even though I had bought in seemingly half a lifetime quantities before my chemotherapy. She will help me get those groceries into the house. The wonderful thing about Sandy's and my friendship is that it is between two people who are givers in life, and that mutual reciprocity makes the relationship very special. Sandy is one of the few people who knew my late husband, Herman, because we were frequent guests at her B&B before we bought our house in Plymouth. She adored my clown of a husband, but she has been equally supportive of my longer-term goal of finding new love in my life, saying any man would be lucky to have me. So you can understand that, despite any current trial and tribulations, I feel calmer and nourished after a visit to her house, and I know she feels the same about me.

On Sundays, my treat is always talking to my sister via Facetime; it is an hour each week that I look forward to greatly. My sister Susan is an interesting and intelligent person, having been a judge in the UK for the past 15 years. I never tire hearing about her cases at work, and of course updates about her family. I have no family in the USA, and it helps to not feel so alone in the world. Also, recently I have been watching some Sunday British PBS shows on television. I do not watch television very much and during chemotherapy could not even concentrate enough to watch it. So something as seemingly mundane as watching TV again is actually a big treat.

Late Sunday afternoon, but before my Sunday TV respite, I drove (yes I drove!) my friend Rose to the beach to eat at a very casual establishment, whose cooking of fish is simple but quite delicious. Rose is a splendid woman who neither looks nor acts her age, although she could be my mother. Driving to this restaurant becomes a little rugged at the end of the beach road, but being able to eat on the beach as the sun is setting, and with the waves lapping a few feet away, is undeniably the sweetness of summer, which is all too fleeting in New England. It was also a treat for Rose, who is a very elegant lady, but was game enough to rough it on the beach. I am very close to Rose who, like Sandy, listens without judgement and gives me remarkably good common sense advice. She understands the grief and loss felt by being widowed, and was one of the first people to outstretch a helping hand after Herman's death. She is my role model for how I want to end up when I am her age. While not as spry as she used to be, there is nothing wrong with her brain and her courage in losing her husband after nearly 60 years of marriage is quite remarkable. Rose has a full social life, although like me she feels very acutely the loss of love and a partner in life. And so it was on early Sunday evening, we ate a fish dinner on the beach and enjoyed the simpler pleasures of life.

Lesson learned: Even in the darkest of times, take some time to be good to yourself. You would be amazed at how much it can lift your mood.

WORKING TOGETHER
August 15th, 2014

Jon and I have had huge breakthroughs in working together, even just over the last week, and we both acknowledged the shift. Suddenly all his coaching for my business started to make some sense.

I went back to review my notes of previous meetings with him, homework I did for him, etc. Quite clearly, almost everything we worked on together this past week has been said many times before, but somehow I was understanding it differently. I shook my head. Had I been that dense?

The answer that came to me was that, until now, I was dutifully participating in conversations with him, but with the left side of my brain only. It was simply an academic exercise with nothing fitting together in a cohesive whole for me. I was way too sick and in pain to do anything else. This is not an excuse, but a statement of where I was; I didn't care. The life force needed to rise up and lead my company again simply wasn't in me. So I would write down his words, tried my best to comply and do homework, but it was empty, as my emotions and heart were not involved. My emotions were involved in managing my health, plain and simple.

Only when I finally got in touch emotionally with the difference that my company used to make in people's lives, the improvements in their health, could I fully engage and believe I could lead again and fight for something that is really worthwhile. I have probably told you more than once that I lead my life from my heart. It would be easier if I did not.

Since the fallout from a CFO and the internal financial shenanigans, my life at the company has recently been all about dollars and I have hated it. Every time I have created a new website in the past, whether it was about allergies, sleep, green living, or pain, it was because it was something I believed in passionately. When, during Jon's and my discussions, we moved the context of my business from increasing sales to doing the right thing for the customer and improving their health, and trusting that the money would follow, a weight lifted off my back.

It was hard to explain to Jon, but it was the best I could do. There have been times in my life when I have been financially successful, but the money was a byproduct of doing something of value for humanity. That will never change about me.

Lesson learned: I may be a businesswoman, but it is not money that drives me. I have always known that but lost sight of that for a while.

ON BEING A HERO AND INSPIRATION?
August 16th, 2014

I get feedback all the time on Facebook, and from cards I get from people, that they see me as inspirational, their leader and hero. One woman repeated that message in a card she sent me today, but said she knew I did not feel that way about myself. It is true that I do not see myself as a hero. I wonder if anybody does about themselves? I am both honored and humbled by the accolades. All I see in myself is a woman whose life has served up to her a number of real curve balls in the last few years, and who just puts one foot wearily in front of the other, dealing with them as best she can. Isn't that what we all try to do—our best?

I know it has been said over the years that I inspire others. While I feel honored that I can clearly make a difference in others' lives, and have tried to do so my entire life, nevertheless, that perception of me still holds puzzlement. Please understand, if you met me, you would find a mildly introverted person who does not seek the limelight and is not endowed with oodles of sparkling charisma. I quietly go about my business, just trying to be a good friend to those I find along my path. I am very awkward and shy in groups of strangers, although with age I have managed to cover it up, at least to some degree.

Many millions of women before me have suffered breast cancer, and I know of others with far worse cases than mine. Still more others have illnesses that makes mine look like a pale shadow compared to what they are going through. While the stress I am feeling right now about my business keeps me up at night, I am terrified, but I am not at the poverty line. So why see me as a hero or inspirational? I confess to feeling like a fraud.

DARE TO DREAM
August 24th, 2014

I have always dreaded so-called retirement. A life just filled with golf and bridge, however delightful diversions I might have at the time, has always seemed like a purposeless and empty life. At least with my company, AllergyBuyersClub.com, I have known that I was making a difference in the health and wellbeing of others. But after 15 years, and the stresses of the past couple of years, it no longer gives me the same joy, mostly because of the financial responsibility that goes along with it. The financial burden is at times exquisitely painful, and keeps me up at night.

One of the things I reflected on after recently watching the television program Mind over Medicine was about those things that gave me joy in life, and one of them is certainly giving to others. When I went down memory lane, I could see that some of the highest points of my life and some of the sweetest memories had to do with giving to other people. So I asked myself the question, supposing by some miracle I became wealthy and found a way to help others in need, would I become happy again and would I have healed my life? The answer, which was a resounding "yes," was startling in its clarity.

But before I dream of the future, I am going to take a look back at the times when giving of myself in some way, whether it be time or money, made a difference in others' lives and enriched my own in the process. My purpose in doing so is not to boast about how great or generous a person I am, far from it—there are countless others whose selfless generosity puts mine to shame. Rather, as I sit in my own current financial and health crises, I am trying to envision for myself a life after cancer that is worth living, and one in which I am healed and the cancer will never return.

It is easiest to be generous and give to those you are closest to, and my first acts of generosity were to my family.

Mother's Kitchen

My mother was an incredible cook. Her kitchen was lined with dozens of cookery books, jars of herbs and spices, and homemade preserves such as marmalade or raspberry jam. The kitchen was my mother's castle, where she as queen reigned supreme. It was the source of creations that rivaled some of the dishes from the best chefs' kitchens in London. My mother was particularly fortunate, as she had collected cooking tips from countless London chefs over half a lifetime—a direct benefit of one of my father's side jobs as a weekly restaurant critic and writer. My mother would spend countless hours experimenting in the kitchen, and my father and the rest of the family were the happy recipients of her experiments. But our kitchen at home was tiny and cramped, its appliances were outdated, the cabinets' paint was chipped, and, like any great cook, my mother was envious of friends with beautiful kitchens.

My mother's sixtieth birthday coincided with a time when I had just received a modest entrepreneurial windfall. And so I arrived in England with an announcement and a check to update the kitchen. I did not have unlimited money, so it was indeed a budget kitchen, but it was enough to allow my mother to have the kitchen of her dreams. I remember the surprise and the thrill it gave her, not the least of which was the months of planning for the design and expansion of her favorite room in the house. Years afterwards, I would walk into that kitchen and it made me smile as I saw my mother pottering around in her retirement. She was a cook who delighted in her new home.

The Dream Vacation

My mother got breast cancer at 65 years old and had a radical mastectomy on one breast. I flew to London to help my father take care of her. It was now my turn to cook, and I cooked like a demon for a week, filling a freezer full of neatly labeled meals, allowing my father to microwave a different variety of meal each day for the next two months. I had a rotation of at least eight different dishes. But for all that, what concerned me most was seeing my mother lie in bed, so obviously in pain and depressed. She knew that six weeks of radiation would come soon after she had healed from surgery. She confessed that she felt she had nothing to look forward to in life. That confession saddened me. This time my fortunes were at an all time low, but I suddenly remembered that I had never closed one bank account in England, and it had lain for over ten years untouched, except for supplying my needs for purchasing a few gifts or expenses on my trips to London. So one day I checked on the balance of that bank account, and discovered it still had a few thousand dollars in it. Then I went to a local travel agent to collect brochures of trips all around the world. I arrived home one day, sat on the edge of my mother's bed and deposited a huge stack of travel literature on her bedside table. "Happy Reading," I told her, and announced that she could choose a vacation for two anywhere in the world within certain budgetary limits. The change in my mother was quite remarkable. She spent hours poring over the travel material that I had provided her, and by the end of my stay had chosen her dream vacation, two weeks at a five-star hotel in Madeira. This was a place she had always wanted to visit. When she was going through the slog of weeks of daily radiation, she told me later that it was the thought of the vacation at the end that had kept her going. I smiled when I heard that—my gift had done its job.

The Car

My first ever employee at AllergyBuyersClub.com, Mary Jo, walked into my office one day in great consternation. Her car had been totaled and she did not know how she was going to scrape together the money for a new one. At the time, the company was still very much a start-up, and we surely did not have a lot of extra cash, but we did have some. So I impulsively pulled out my checkbook and wrote a check, enough for the outright purchase of a new car. Mary Jo's eyes filled with tears and I smiled. What else is money good for except to share your good fortune with those you love?

The Vet

Some years later I walked past the cubicle of another employee, Heather, and saw she had tears streaming down her face, and I asked her why. The reason, I was told, was that her cat, scarcely more than a kitten, had been hit by a car the night before. She was distraught. The vet had told her that the cat could be saved through an operation costing several thousand dollars. Heather did not know how she could even begin to afford such a sum. Being the consummate cat lover, this story touched my heart. Once again, I pulled out the corporate checkbook and took care of the bill. With both these incidents with my employees, we never spoke of them again, and they were instructed not to talk about them to their coworkers. But in each case, I smiled when I made out those checks. There is joy in giving.

Africa

My safari trip was one of the most unusual of my giving adventures—for an adventure this surely was. Before my trip I had heard of the extreme poverty in Africa, and indeed had witnessed it firsthand as a child. A friend who recently had been on a safari told me to bring with me small gifts of toiletries, pens or toys to give away when we visited African villages. She also told me to wear old clothes and just leave them behind at each hotel. I really warmed to this idea and my husband was signed up for 25 pounds of hand luggage stuffed full of useful items, including fake designer watches! And I did the same. When we met our guide in Kenya, I told him we would appreciate a visit to a couple of extra villages in addition to our itinerary, since I had gifts for the villagers, especially the children.

At each village, I solemnly bowed to the chief and gave him a fake watch, which I knew he could trade for food for his village; pens that lit up in the dark provided light at night where there was no electricity; and high bouncing balls brought shrieks of delight to young children. Toiletries, which I saved from each hotel, were sent to a local orphanage.

I learned that American visitors were welcomed in these villages because of their donations. But I was distressed to hear that for a number of years, following a terrorist attack in Nairobi, President Bush had advised Americans not to go to Kenya. So no American visitors came to these villages for several years, and the people in the villages and their cattle simply starved. I felt like a big fat ugly spoiled American. I felt very ashamed of my affluence.

I remember very clearly one recipient of my hand luggage booty. He served in a hotel gift shop and we fell to talking about his life. In order to earn a living, he lived 200 miles away from his wife and he was helping his daughter attend college, although he wasn't sure whether she could continue to attend because of the cost. That man received a number of my watches and pens, and I said that I hoped that when he sold them it would go to pay his daughter's tuition. Imagine my surprise, some six months later, when I got a letter from his daughter thanking me for my generosity, saying it had paid for over one semester of her college fees. That made me smile.

Our trip was an all inclusive one, tips included, but I carried a large number of one dollar bills. After each meal I left one or two dollars behind for our servers. My tips, which were equivalent to a day's pay, provoked numerous conversations with the Africans who were waiting on us. I learned so much about them and their culture. I found them to be wonderful people. Leaving them and their beautiful animals had me crying when I left Nairobi. It was the trip of a lifetime and moved me deeply.

Returns

One of the things that happens each month in a retail establishment is we get returns of perfectly good merchandise. People just change their minds, and we have no viable second-hand outlet. So what I have done over the years is to surprise a lot of people. Countless friends who were in need received anything from a new mattress, air purifier, vacuum cleaner, dehumidifier, humidifier or steam cleaner and the like. Certainly items that most of them would not be able to buy for themselves, and never the same quality. It always makes me smile when I see my friends pick out something that contributes to their health and wellbeing. Other samples and returns have been donated to many deserving strangers or charity auctions. One of the favorite events at my company is a raffle of all these accumulated goods. Some employees give these wonderful products to their families for Christmas gifts. Others have sold items on eBay to earn a bit of extra money. The raffle is eagerly awaited by staff and we hype it up a bit so that it's good fun for everyone. For one raffle, which was not attended by employees I had sponsored a summer-long weekend retreat summer for caregivers and widows of people who have suffered through brain cancer. I had arranged for a number of renewing activities throughout the weekend, and everyone stayed as guests in my friends' homes, but the grand finale was a raffle where each attendee got to pick three items from a long list, and I paid to have the items shipped to their homes. I am very fortunate to have been able to give away many hundreds of thousands of dollars worth of healthy-living products over the years, and it gives me far more pleasure than putting the goods in the hands of a liquidator. I have sometimes mourned the thought of selling my business as, if nothing else, I would be deprived of the pleasure of giving these goods away.

My Jewelry

Sometimes I am a bit embarrassed when I want to be generous to others. About ten years ago, my husband Herman had dug deep into his pocket to give me a diamond pendant. I was so moved by his generosity that I told him I would wear it every day. Its simplicity appealed to me, and the love behind the gift moved me greatly. But then, since I was going to wear that pendant every day, what was I going to do with the rest of my jewelry, which surely would go unworn? I embarked on a huge audit of my wardrobe, both for my clothes and jewelry. Quite frankly, I was rather ashamed. I had far too much "stuff". I wore only a fraction of my wardrobe. So I did a grand clearance and arrived one day at work with three shopping bags teeming with expensive jewelry. Beautiful things, but rarely worn. I enrolled Susan, one of my employees who made jewelry as a hobby, to decide which employees should get which pieces of jewelry and to distribute them for me. I did the same with a number of my clothes. Of course, some of my employees wondered whether I was terminally ill, but I smiled when I saw some of my jewelry or clothes walking around the office. Far better that they should all get pleasure from them than collecting dust in my closet.

Closing House

When I closed up my house in Newton before moving to my summer home in Plymouth full time, I was faced with a dilemma. I had two of everything, because the summer home was completely furnished. I debated whether I wanted to have a house sale like I had held over a decade ago, after moving from a very large house, but decided against it. Rather, this time, except for a few beautiful antique pieces, I was going to give the stuff away. I knew enough about my employees' lives to know which ones could do with a new couch, washer-dryer or bed, and made offers to them. The rest was a free for all where they could help themselves. It was much more satisfying than selling my household goods to strangers.

Cooking

In recent times, I have been living a more modest lifestyle, but even so, my cooking adventures have been ones that I have shared with friends. After Herman's death I attended cooking school, rediscovering food that I really enjoyed, trying out new recipes and discovering new favorites. Having found it difficult to make recipes for just one person, I have made it a habit of cooking on Sundays in winter and then distributing my dishes to friends in need. There never seems to be a shortage of people amongst my personal circle who, for one reason or another, were finding it difficult to cook. There is something about home cooked food that is incredibly nurturing.

Conclusion

My point in telling you these stories is to help myself on my healing journey. I do not see myself as especially generous, but I do enjoy giving to others. Writing this down publicly for the first time has helped me recognize the part of life that gives me joy. It is giving to others. What will the butterfly do when she finally emerges from the cocoon and flies free once more? She will have a giving aspect to her life.

Lesson learned: There is so much joy in giving and I am blessed by being a natural giver. It comes easily to me. Therefore, in knowing that about myself, when I emerge from my life in the cocoon, there will surely be some form of giving incorporated into it.

HEALTH UPDATE
August 24th, 2014

The side effects from chemo are receding fast now that I am two and a half months out of chemotherapy, and I am also healing from surgery nicely, which was now six weeks ago. I still have pain and restricted movement under my left arm. My hair is very slowly coming back, dead straight and salt and pepper. Unfortunately, more salt than pepper! Oh well. The residual effect that I still struggle with most is massive fatigue. I never wake up feeling refreshed and vital in the morning and because of the stress in my life at work, it takes a great deal of self discipline to get going each day. It is only just over a week before I start radiation, so I am trying hard in my business and personal life to get as much done as possible before the next wave of fatigue really hits me. I keep telling myself that by mid-October that I will be done with the bulk of my treatment and then I can truly work on healing my life. I look out onto the golf course and say: "Maybe next year..."

THE NEXT PHASE LOOMS
August 28th, 2014

The next phase of my treatment is nearly upon me. I start radiation on September 2nd; it will be every day for seven weeks. I have now been for both radiation mapping and simulation appointments, and I confess that I haven't gotten used to the whole process yet. Today when I came out of simulation, Jon was waiting for me and gave me a big hug, and I found myself choking back the tears; it was such a relief to be out of the radiation room. In truth, I find it rather scary. I am also coming to terms with the reality that radiation fatigue occurs in the second half of treatment and, for the following weeks after treatment, is pretty brutal, so I have to redesign my life accordingly. At our staff meeting today, Jon told my staff not to expect to see much of me during October. With so much to do at work, the idea of having no energy at such a critical time is killing me. It is very difficult to find any enthusiasm for this next phase. I am only starting to get some mobility and energy back after surgery, and now I will slowly go downhill again. I keep telling myself, October 17th will be over soon, and I will be on the home stretch. But right now seven weeks away seems like an eternity.

THIS WAS THE WEEK THAT WAS
August 29th, 2014

Another tumultuous week has passed, where I wake up at the end of it and say: "Thank goodness that is over!" With radiation starting next week, every day for seven weeks, I suspect I will be saying that quite frequently.

Jon is in town this week helping me with my business. Monday was a very tough day, as I needed to put almost the last of my dwindling funds into the company. He and I both hated to see that happen, and on Monday the pressure he was putting on me to produce sales results out of thin air became unbearable, and we could hardly speak to each other that evening. I felt trapped with nowhere to go. I had also shared with Jon that I thought it prudent to immediately start the process of putting the company up for sale. By Tuesday morning over breakfast, he shared that it was eating his heart out to see me having to put more funds into the company. We held hands over the breakfast table with tears in our eyes and I realized that his ill humor of the day before derived from his caring and concern for me. From then on, we worked well together for the rest of the week where bad news on the business front mounted daily.

Yet for all that, there were some chinks of light. Somehow, miraculously out of nowhere on Tuesday, we started to get some unsolicited interest in the business from multiple sources, and Jon began to feel that we did indeed have something of value to sell. We agreed that selling a company is a full-time job for a CEO at the best of times and I would be better off letting somebody else take the reins for a while, so that the growth initiatives of the business could still proceed, which of course is imperative. Add the fatigue factor, which is highly likely from the radiation, and it was clear that I could not grow the company, return it to profitability, sell the company and cope with health challenges at the same time. Even superwoman has her limitations. As Jon and I started to map out a course of action for the next few months, we stood shoulder to shoulder tackling some of the numerous day-to-day missiles that were flying past our ears.

ONE WEEK DOWN, SIX TO GO
September 6th, 2014

There was really no choice this week but to put my big girl panties on and start daily radiation. I had to smile when I heard the song "Big Girls Don't Cry" over the PA system at the hospital. That just about sums it up. Unfortunately for me, I am one of those fair skinned rare birds whose bodies protest at being radiated. I went pink and puffed up within 24 hours, a reaction not usually seen for two weeks. The doctor said I might be one of those few people who may need to take a treatment break at some point in order to heal, and then resume treatment later. Just what I needed to hear. Meanwhile, I have to slather myself with deep moisturizer multiple times a day.

At this point my energy level is pretty normal, and any fatigue I feel is more due to nearly four hours of driving each day, and the stress at work, which is just over the top as I struggle for survival.

But for all this, as my friend Rose remarked this morning, I really have an extraordinary number of people who care about me. It is a source of constant amazement to me, although Rose said she wasn't at all surprised. Life is really all about love in the end, and in that regard I feel very blessed.

I went to the cemetery yesterday to pay my respects, as the anniversary of Herman's death approaches, since on the actual day I will be tied up at hospital. The night before, I had closed my eyes before I put my hand into a basket of memorial stones. I wondered if the message from Heaven was going to be "courage," so I wasn't surprised when I pulled out the courage stone. As I sat by his graveside, I thought about the extraordinary courage that Herman had exhibited in facing his brain cancer. I appreciate that depth of courage far more today than I did then. But I also thought that the message was for me, to be courageous and take heart, that it will all work out in the end. As I prayed by his graveside, I received the message that, by the end of next week, there would be miracles in my life that would leave me smiling. We shall see. I certainly need divine intervention.

Lesson learned: Courage is rising up again to fight when there seems no reason to do so. Take heart that your fight will take you to a better place.

THE RADIATION ROOM
September 12th, 2014

You can hear a pin drop in the radiation waiting room. We all know why we are here; we are fighting for our lives. Sons, daughters, and husbands are in solicitous attendance, hovering anxiously over their loved ones, often stroking their hands. We lone valiant soldiers steal sympathetic glances at each other. "What number are you on?" we whisper, and wish each other good luck. Once in a while, a loud bell clangs and clapping is heard, someone has finally got to the end of their treatment. But for the most part, we sit silently and wait for the radiation technician, who signals us quietly to follow her.

After a while you get to know the drill. You are required to hold your breath when given the "breathe in and out" signal over the intercom from the technicians, safely housed in a room across the hallway. The machine moves itself around you, zapping you from different positions and for different durations. But you and the machine are alone. As one lady told me in the ladies' room: this is your own private journey, and you try not to think about how scary it is.

Two down and five weeks to go.

DIVINE GUIDANCE

I wake up each morning to a new despair,
I ask God, tell me when will I come up for air?
He tells me, all happens for a reason
And take heart, life has its season.
I ask for divine guidance to show me the way
So that I can truly live another day.

Mercia Tapping

YES, MIRACLES DID HAPPEN LAST WEEK
September 14th, 2014

I prayed at Herman's gravesite a week ago for miracles to happen through divine intervention. I was at an all time low. Turned out that last week my angel truly pulled out all the stops for me.

The week began miserably enough, but on Wednesday the tide began to turn. One of my vendors appeared to visit ostensibly about a strategic alliance, but it turned out to be a formal presentation as to why they should acquire my business. He had clearly done his research, and the synergies in company missions and pathways for expansion of my company was very attractive. Jon was present at the meeting, helping with my response, and was introduced as my acting president to run the company during my illness. Of course, the vendor found him very impressive and remarked that post acquisition he would like us both to stay on. Next day, Jon talked to him some more while I was in hospital getting radiation. I was buoyed by the time I met them both for lunch. Our first prospective buyer had miraculously shown up, and then later that day, I got news that another vendor wanted to speak to me on Friday for the same reason. Maybe all was not lost.

On Thursday, I spoke to two investment bankers introduced to me via a friend. This time I really became encouraged. I had been thinking that our deal was too small to be of interest to investment bankers, but I was pleasantly surprised. Both bankers said that any number of acquiring companies would find us a very attractive proposition, and the losses in my company were pretty minimal, and entirely understandable given the extenuating circumstances. The intrinsic value of the company was still there and both bankers would be delighted to take me on as a client.

By the end of the week, I could not believe the abundance of miracles. There were now three companies who wanted to throw their hat into the ring when the company goes out to formal bid via the investment banker. I had found a female investment banker who usually deals with larger transactions, but who was so moved by my story and intrigued by the company that she wanted me as a client. I liked her and go by my instincts. And then there was Jon, who was now the acting president of my company. There is a saying that God works in mysterious ways. I could see the hand of God in my life this week, and I was profoundly grateful. My weekend began with my ability to actually get a reasonable night's sleep, and with Jon now formally at the helm as acting company president, I could feel the crushing stress begin to lighten.

Lesson learned: Miracles can happen in your darkest hours, especially if you pray for them.

GOOD SOLDIER
September 20th, 2014

I would characterize myself this last week as being a good soldier trudging to radiation every day. I can feel radiation fatigue slowly but surely creeping up on me, and I will be relieved when my team of volunteer drivers start on Monday. Afternoon naps are occurring more often, and I frequently find myself yawning and making steps towards the bedroom as early as 8 p.m. This does not make me the life of the party! I am now over one third through radiation and by mid next week I will have reached the halfway mark. I cross off each day on my radiation wall calendar and remind myself that this is September and I have been in treatment all year; miraculously I am nearing the finish line.

Jon was here in Boston all week slaying dragons at the company on my behalf and somehow keeping everything going. I watched in amazement as he tackled all the sacred cows of processes that I have been in favor of changing for a long while, but failed to get any staff buy-in. Now, as our new acting company president, he just tackled those issues head on, taking no prisoners. It has left some of my staff gasping for breath and certainly has not garnered Jon the warm, fuzzy teddy bear of the year award.

So both of us have been weary at the end of the day, and cooking and having dinner together has been a simple but very meaningful pleasure. The energy between us is just easy, the conversation flows effortlessly, and we raise our glasses up to a better future. Jon always does the dishes after a meal—it's the first time anyone has cleaned up the kitchen for me my entire life. It is the little things he does for me that makes me feel so well cared for.

THE ROAD AHEAD

The wagon wheels roll forward, clack clack,
On this road no turning back,
Dust flies and bites my eyes, I cannot see,

Dear God, what is to become of me?
The answer lies in the road ahead,
Hope springs eternal, it is often said,
Hope is the driver of this road of ours,
I look to the side, smile and see the flowers.

Mercia Tapping

ON ADVERSITY
September 21st, 2014

My massage therapist, who has known me for several years, told me that he was betting on me to rise up again. He said that I had no idea of how strong a woman I was, and how he had seen me face each challenge of the last few years with such grace and courage. He then startled me by saying that he had seen multiple people in similar circumstances commit suicide. That remark took me aback. What makes one person survive and triumph over adversity while another person fails?

I thought about the example my parents had set for me as a child, with my father, a professional man, sometimes facing unemployment. During each financial setback my parents faced together, and pulled through, they never appeared sorry for themselves. And I remember, to my amazement, my mother taking a job for a short while as a lady's maid in London, so I could continue to go to private school. She had come from a family that was quite affluent, but she always did what was needed to support my father through the ups and downs of his career. And if it meant pinching pennies and stretching our grocery bill, she did it without complaint.

I did not grow up with a silver spoon in my mouth. Rather, I was taught lessons in resilience and self sufficiency. At ten years old, I got very little pocket money, far less than my classmates, so I got a job as a papergirl riding around on my bike at 5:30 a.m. delivering newspapers. Getting my tips at Christmas was a thrill, and allowed me to put some gifts for my family underneath the sparsely populated Christmas tree, which we waited until Christmas Eve to buy when the prices fell.

I am sure that those early years set the stage for who I am today. Beaten down and bloodied for sure, but don't count me out. I will rise again.

Lesson learned: Rise up from adversity and dream of a better life. Do it without complaint.

SLOWING DOWN
September 22nd, 2014

I have four more weeks of daily Monday to Friday radiation and, as of today, a noble group of friends, organized by Maureen, will be shuttling me back and forth each day to MGH. If I surprise myself by having a relatively good day, I will have my driver drop me off at the office and spend the afternoon there, and then Jon can drive me home.

However, after three weeks of radiation the forecasted fatigue is starting, slowly but surely, to catch up with me. Twice this last week, I felt lucky to have driven myself home safely. Over this last weekend I forced myself through my usual weekend chores, when truth be told I just wanted to snooze. I think for a while that my sociability in the evenings will be strictly limited. Even after an afternoon snooze and a hefty belt of Diet Coke, when I went out this weekend to the local community theater and my book group, the pervading and dominant thought in my mind after 8 p.m. was "Lemme out of here, I want to go home and sleep!"

So I will be living a very quiet life, only making rare appearances at work for the next month. The radiation ends Friday, October 17th, and its after effects are said to last a good 4-6 weeks. However, after radiation is finished I will be back in the office, albeit briefly at first, but building up as my energy levels return.

I keep telling myself, take it one day at a time. In the end, that's all you can do anyway.

Lesson learned: In the midst of one's troubles, take it one day at a time and breathe!

COUNTING BLESSINGS
September 27th, 2014

I know that I am being a good soldier trudging in for daily radiation, and I know that this week I passed the halfway mark, so therefore I am on the homeward stretch. Rationally, I should be almost exultant, But emotionally I am spent, I am exhausted and I have immense debilitating shoulder pain from acute bursitis, which stabs me like sharp knives at every turn. So it is becoming harder to get out of bed in the mornings, and I hate that my afternoons seem to be consumed with long naps. It seems like such a boring waste of life. I do so long for this all to be over and to feel normal again.

It is in times like these that I force myself to count my blessings. I use the word "force" advisedly, because part of me wants to wallow in a pity party. But the warrior part of me is determined not to let the cancer beast get the best of me. I am truly a blessed and lucky woman. I mean that quite seriously.

- The sun is shining and I sit and look out onto an incredible view of the golf course.
- One of my cats sleeps curled up next to me purring contentedly.
- I am in the hands of some of the best doctors in the world, who root for my recovery at every turn.
- I avoided a full mastectomy and my surgeon did an amazing job, so I am not unduly misshapen.
- My company is now headed by Jon as its acting president, taking the stress off my back, and staffed by my loyal employees.
- I have been connected with an excellent investment banker to represent me in the sale of my company, and we have nibbles of interest already, before we go to market for auction.
- I have a huge group of friends organized as a team of drivers ferry-

ing me back and forth to Mass General each day, and I am delight-ing in the conversations in the car with friends, whom I am getting to know in new ways.

- My tastebuds are back and food never tasted so good!
- And yes, my hair is growing back at last! It is baby soft and I never tire of stroking it.
- My girlfriends, especially Sandy and Rose, make sure that I am not lonely at weekends.
- My massage therapist even sees me on Sundays while I am under-going cancer treatment.

For all this I am truly blessed.

Lesson learned: If you make a practice of sitting down and listing your blessings, you will feel immeasurably better.

WHY BOTHER?
September 28th, 2014

As the radiation weeks churn on, in the still of the night that little voice whispers: "Why bother? What do you really have to live for?" Do not think for a moment that this is the voice of suicide; rather, it is a vexing question and a search for meaning in the next phase of my life. There is a part of me that is curiously sad about my decision to sell my company. I am not ending with a roar, more like a whimper. No blaze of glory, just memories of happier times at work instead of the struggles of the last five years. I am very bored, nursing my fatigue and my swollen, reddened breast. I cannot for a moment envisage being a lady of leisure with nothing more than a social calendar. I wonder where this book will take me? Will it inspire people? Will people want to hear me speak from the podium once more? What is the message I want to impart? At the moment, I cannot rightly tell you. What I do know is life has to have a purpose larger than one's own disease or grief. And one has to have the faith that one can create life to be the way one wants it to be, and a phoenix can rise from the ashes. So how will my phoenix take shape? How is my final legacy to the world going to manifest itself before I gracefully exit stage left?

Lesson learned: The answer to "Why bother to fight for your life?" lies outside your natural selfish desire to live. It lies outside yourself and is bigger than your own life, because your living will impact the lives of many.

LOVE AND ILLNESS
October 4th, 2014

I am reminded that, seven months ago in a visitation from Herman, he gave me a message with the Ace of Hearts that: "Love would be my protection, love would be my guide and love would be my reward."

At the time, I surely felt his love beaming down from Heaven, but I had little idea of the deeply transformative path I would be taking, as I experienced love and kindness from an ever-widening circle of friends and the community at large. I feel loved and cared for by numerous people every day, and under the force of such fierce love, my heart has broken open at the miracles of love that I am being so freely given. I have never experienced directly and so profoundly the goodness in humanity. It is humbling and joyful. The joyful part is that I am not only the recipient of an enormous wealth of love and compassion, but the walls I have felt between myself and others over my entire life are melting away. As a teenager, under the stresses of female bitchiness in boarding school, I learned to protect myself from verbal barbs, and I think my time there created a part of me that was afraid of what others might think or say of me. It developed into what is known as "English Reserve." Certainly, even before my illness, I had already become far more emotionally accessible as I have aged, especially enveloped in the security and love of my marriage with Herman. But my circle of love was very constricted, and Herman used to worry endlessly about who would look after me when he was gone.

My illness brought me to my knees, and to the point where I desperately needed help from others, and those close to me recognized that need immediately. As the worst phase of my battle with cancer is nearly over and within sight, I can admit that I have never felt so sick in my entire life, and it will have consumed most of 2014. The idea that I might need others to cook, drive, clean, do errands, help me with personal care, let alone run my business for me, was simply an idea that had never entered my head. I was used to being self contained, independent, and resilient. But it was in the vulnerability of being ill that I learned to receive love and to be open to loving so many more in return.

The humbling part of all this is difficult to describe. In many ways, I feel such an unworthy recipient of so much love. I do not feel entitled to it, yet when offered loving acts, much like a saving branch being offered to a man being swept downstream by dark swirling waters, I latch onto that branch, almost greedily but certainly gratefully. Without this love from others, I surely would have drowned.

My life this year has been a tapestry of "loving moments," and each one holds a certain sweetness and joy even in the midst of my physical challenges. It may be a strange thing to say, but I think that this year, in retrospect, will have held more "loving moments" than at any prior time in my life. There have been many hundreds of such moments, but I share with you just a few which come to mind, and in no particular order:

- Linda appeared like an unexpected angel, a blyth spirit in my life taking me to so many chemo appointments. I will never forget her racing through the halls of Mass General with me in a wheelchair, drugged up to my eyeballs on morphine, my clutching her gift of flowers, and her flirting and waving to every man who opened the doors for us. This was truly a sight to behold. Linda always had a little thoughtful gift for me on chemo days and managed to make me laugh, even when I was receiving an infusion of the "Red Devil," the most brutal of all my chemo infusions.

- Sandy has just been a ministering angel, pouring love on me when I have been at my sickest. There is really no other way to describe it. I stayed at her house twice post-chemotherapy infusions and she brought me hot or cold compresses, tempted my appetite when I could hardly eat or swallow, and figured out natural remedies as my immune system crumbled and I got one kind of infection after another. She responded to my wailing, self-pitying texts late at night, and cooked me endless meals when the will to cook for myself eluded me. Sometimes, she made lightning fast visits to my house to change my bed linen, clean up cat litter or cat vomit, all with a smile on her face, when she has so much on her plate, already looking after her husband who has Alzheimer's. We have eaten together, cried together, laughed together and prayed for a better future for us both next year.

- And then there is Rose, in her mid-eighties, who checks up on me daily. Rose has cooked me endless meals, even when I was so destroyed by chemotherapy I could hardly lift my fork to my mouth and my face all but fell onto my plate. She has been endlessly patient and encouraging as I have confided to her my woes, my fears and my aspirations for the future. Who would ever think I would develop such a loving relationship with a woman some nearly 20 years my senior? Yet it is one of the sweetest and most precious relationships in my life.

- Debbie, who has a nursing background, but whom I only knew casually before my illness, has been one of those people who has been the bravest of all. She accompanied me to important decision-making doctor's appointments about my next phases of treatment, and tended my wounds after surgery until I became more comfortable with emptying my drains. She has brought me flowers to brighten my days, and turkey pies from a local farm when my appetite needed tempting during chemo. Getting to know Debbie has been such a delightful collateral side benefit of my illness, and a reminder of how many wonderful, loving people there are right on my doorstep.

- Of course, I expected my medical team at a hospital like Mass General to be top notch in their competency. What was unexpected was the number of doctors and nurses who have hugged me, comforted me and held one of my hands in theirs. I have not felt like a patient with a number around them. I am a human being that they value and want to see restored to health.

- Sometimes the loving moments appear out of the blue. My cleaning lady has left me beautiful personally designed flower arrangements; others have sent me fruit, flowers, cards, a phone conversation, a thoughtful food treat, or prayer bears that seem to arrive just when I am struggling to rise above my daily physical and emotional challenges. It is those smiles and hugs that I get at my pharmacy, my dry cleaners or local restaurants that I patronize, which remind me that this is not a journey that I am taking alone, and that I am loved.

- So many people, including friends on Facebook, tell me that they pray for me on a daily or weekly basis. It seems an extraordinary privilege to be included on people's prayer list, and comforting to know all those people truly want me to recover. I appreciate the love that lies behind those prayers.

- As I write this, I have a team of dedicated drivers who ferry me up and down to Boston on a daily basis for my radiation. They all give up their time selflessly for me, knowing that, as the weeks progress, it gets to be more challenging for me. Each person expresses their caring for me differently, but the conversations in the car are an unexpected pleasure. The gift of time allows for conversations that we in our busy lives seem to no longer have time for. I learn about their children and grandchildren, family illnesses, fears, hopes and dreams as well as sweet memories from their earlier lives. We all know that I am fighting for my life, so the conversations are both uplifting but meaningful, certainly not idle chatter or complaints about trivial irritations. I look at these car rides and conversations as an unexpected and loving gift.

It is through this extended community of love that I am being left in a place where I no longer fear my fellow humans; I embrace them and love them. It is that love we share that will sustain me through this and guide me to the expression of the next phase of my life. I think I am finally seeing the light at the end of this grim tunnel.

Lesson learned: Look for the abundance of loving moments in your life because they will nourish you.

LOVE IS MY GUIDE

Love is my guide and comfort in a sea of desolation,
The waves of despair crash against the shore
The salty wind whipping my face as I cry for deliverance.
Love stretches out its hand to comfort me.
Friends offer prayers, hope, and a meal that warms my belly.
A hug holds the promise of human warmth.
Laughter is a precious, joyful moment.
Love infuses itself through my chilled body as if to resuscitate me
And give me courage to face another day.

Mercia Tapping

PAIN AND SUFFERING
October 5th, 2014

No one welcomes pain and illness into their lives, and for those of us who qualify for senior discounts, it is an unkind reminder that our bodies do not work as well as they once did, and we slowly face our own mortality. One thing is for certain, at some point we will die. It is all too tempting to remember how we had boundless energy, ran around with gay abandon, burned the candle at both ends, and perhaps participated in some sport, pushing our bodies to some physical zenith. Then illness and pain rudely interrupts, and we suffer because we cannot accept the reality of the present. We so desperately wish it was some other way.

I never fell into the trap of wondering "Why Me?" when I got cancer, but I have certainly sat in some horror and been puzzled as to how my almost perfect life had changed so dramatically over the past 5-6 years. It is in the rebellion against "what is," the non-acceptance of reality, and the incessant yearning for change that is the source of suffering, which is very different from physical pain. This is not to say that you should not look forward, as in my case, to a life unburdened by cancer. But as I have said in discussing "loving moments," if your whole focus is thinking about your pain, and not finding value and joy in the present while accepting the current physical challenges you have been presented with, then suffering will surely ensue. It is your thoughts and interpretation of reality that have you suffer.

Right now I am in my last two weeks of radiation. When people ask how I am doing, I reply that, of course, I am weary and my breast is red and swollen like a football and itches like crazy. But I also cheerfully tell them it could be a lot worse, and that so far I am not so tired as I imagined. I also tell them that for someone so fair skinned, thankfully I have managed to avoid burn ointment and, fingers crossed, will be able to get to the end of my treatment without a break. However uncomfortable it is, I tell myself that this too shall pass, and it will be over soon and then I can begin healing. Accepting the present, but knowing that I will heal soon, gives me peace.

Lesson learned: This too shall pass. How many times does this dumb human have to relearn the same lesson? There is only the present.

ONE WEEK LEFT
October 10th, 2014

On October 17th, in one week, and with four treatments to go out of 33, I will finish radiation. My treatment regimen changed today, and I realized they had saved the best for last. It was lengthy, took almost an hour, and was very taxing, so I was pretty shaken up by the end. To be truthful, I had a hard time fighting back the tears. To have to hold perfectly still for almost an hour with both arms above my head, aching like hell, I thought I would scream if treatment didn't end soon! My skin has started to blister, but my radiologist told me she is thankful that my skin has held up as well as it has till now. Apparently in the beginning she was concerned as to whether I could even tolerate the treatment at all, having blown up like a red balloon after the first day. Right now, I understand the true meaning of radiation fatigue; my afternoon naps have slowly progressed to three hours in duration, and I am out cold. I sleep on a towel, since the recommended creams for the breast area are very greasy, and I sleep without a top sheet till the middle of the night when the cream has soaked in and my body has cooled. Quite frankly, each treatment looms daily like a big mountain to climb, but I am blessed with a team of drivers who keep me going, distract me with conversation, and keep me safely off the road. My conversations with my drivers are an unexpected pleasure, affording me the luxury of getting to know friends in a deeper way. But when all is said and done, I will be thankful when this 7-week marathon is over. Then maybe I'll start to get my life back. What a concept! I know it is coming soon, but I have been so deep in my cocoon and for so long, this butterfly has almost forgotten how to fly.

THE RADIATION ROOM

We wait in silence, or perhaps a covert whisper.
The reason why we are there binds us in quiet comradeship.
Each day we trudge, one day more in our battle,

For us, cancer knows no color.
It is a voracious beast that must be stilled.
The machine bears down, whirring, clicking,
As we are told to hold our breath, then breathe.
My face itches and twitches but I still hold still.
And then it is over till tomorrow.
"Good luck," we whisper to the next fellow traveler.
One day, soon, I will ring that bell.
Till then I sleep.

Mercia Tapping

Lesson learned: There is joy in giving, but sometimes you need to let others give to you. My team of drivers were a daily miracle for weeks on end. They gave to me so gracefully. There were even more women who grumbled that they never got on the list! I was made to feel like a rock star, but with endless compassion as I struggled visibly towards the end.

CREATING A NEW LIFE
October 11th, 2014

I have always been good at creating something from nothing, and holding a vision of the seemingly impossible. But I can tell you that as I am now that much older, and my life as I knew it, with a loving husband, flourishing business and perfect health have been ripped away from me, I realize how ephemeral it all is. Even once you achieve your goals, some random event can suddenly intervene and snatch it all away. Curveballs that come from nowhere are life altering.

I remember sitting after my husband had been diagnosed with brain cancer, realizing that my life, let alone his, were never going to be the same. I read about the progression of this hideous disease and felt the deepest of sorrows as I realized that my husband would die like a helpless vegetable, and I would have to bear witness to his daily journey. Even knowing this intellectually ahead of time, I was ill-prepared for the final stages of this disease. No one ever spells it out for you; you are left to discover the horror of it all alone. Such tragedy changes you and, try as I may, I have never found anything redemptive about his death, except to realize that death does indeed come to us all, and we do not choose its time.

My journey as a caregiver had me face that even the strongest amongst us can crack under the strain, and I am left with a deep compassion for caregivers everywhere. Perhaps I am a better person after my caregiving journey? That is hard for me to tell, but deep sorrow makes you treasure even the smallest of joys. And I do not sweat the small stuff anymore, it all seems so trivial by comparison.

When I discovered that my CFO had been presenting me with inaccurate financial reports, and almost all my life savings went to prop up the company, it was another life-altering event. Previously, I had thought that I was running a profitable company and had a nice retirement nest egg. Now my nest egg was gone. That change overnight was my worst nightmare. How on earth could that have happened under my nose? It has left me far more distrustful of others in business world, as I have realized that even the seemingly nicest of people can lie.

Journeying through my own cancer this year is, of course, another life-altering event. I began the year by saying that my life was going to continue as normal and cancer was going to just be an annoyance in the background. Brave, bold words spoken like a true woman warrior, but I had no concept of the depth and breadth of the challenges I would face. Very slowly, but certainly surely, cancer started to take over my life. It was probably for the best that I didn't know what lay before me, since I had to find courage to face each and every day as it presented itself, rather than worrying about the future. Physically, facing my own cancer has been very hard, but mentally facing my husband's cancer was harder. His was a death sentence, whereas mine, God willing, will see me live quite a few more years and disease free.

So the question then becomes, if you have been given a reprieve in life then how do you want to spend it? It certainly isn't to turn the clock back and, of course, one cannot do that anyway. So it has to be something new. But what?

I am reminded of an exercise that I used to give people when I was conducting personal growth courses in a previous career and I will freely share it with you now. The exercise was called "My Successful Twin." The core concept behind the exercise is that your twin is not you, because he or she can have absolutely anything they want in work, love, play, living environment, etc. It is an invitation to dream big. By writing down the life of your successful twin in great detail, it is a message you can send to the universe about what you really want. Over time, the gap between your life and that of your twin will slowly narrow until they become one. It will soon be time for me to write down once again the next chapter in the life of my successful twin. I just need to stagger through to the end of radiation first.

Lesson learned: The shiny new life that I want in my future will need to be created from nothing. As an entrepreneur and visionary, I need to have faith in myself that I can have the life I want and can create it.

DEATH AND THE PHOENIX RISING
October 16th, 2014

I have witnessed the death of three of the closest people to me in life over a 7-year period. Each was more painful than the one preceding it. Each brought me closer to facing my own mortality, and brought with it new depths of sorrow and grief. One thing is surely true, we all need to go through this passage of life. Many of us can probably say that we are wiser and more compassionate to others as a result. But it is clear that the way we deal with the death of our loved ones helps shape the choices we make for the rest of our lives.

The first person to die was my mother. She died of pneumonia at 83 years old in 2003; she had Alzheimer's and was confined to a wheelchair when she died. We let Mother Nature take its course. Her quality of life was no longer there, and we knew she hated being in residential care. Where she spent the last days of her life was like her worst nightmare come true. Seven years before she died, when Alzheimer's had become apparent but her comprehension in the moment was still there, I sent her a thank you letter for everything she had done for me as a mother. My father used to reread the letter to her until she no longer understood its meaning. I knew it was my farewell letter to my mother, since I was well aware of the progression of the disease. The last time I saw her was two years before she died. She was hostile and when I said I was returning to the USA, she said, "good riddance." She spat in my sister's face. I confess that hardly made me want to see her and get rebuffed yet again. It was painful to see her that way. I did, however, spend the last ten days of her life with her as she lay in a coma in the nursing home. It is shocking to admit that she had lost so much weight that I literally did not recognize her, and walked right by her, searching for the mother I once knew. She did acknowledge my presence just once before she died when I asked her to lift a finger if she heard me. It was some small consolation that I knew she heard my words of comfort, and could feel me touching her hand. This was the first time that I understood that death could be, and was, a merciful release. I went back to my life. Ostensibly nothing had changed, but I had become so aware during her illness that health was incredibly precious. This new appreciation of health had formed the cornerstone to my founding AllergyBuyersClub.com. I knew that my business life should clearly reflect my commitment to health. I could not change her health, but maybe I could impact the health of others.

The second person to die was my father, in 2007, and I mourned him for many months. He was the parent to whom I had been closest; now he too was dead and my own mortality loomed large. My second parent was now dead. The family home had been sold a couple of years previously, so I no longer had a home to go to in England. My father died in hospital after a 4-month stay. He arrived with a bladder infection but got MRSA and was diagnosed with Parkinson's. Again, in the end, we let Mother Nature take over.

I had seen my father several times during the preceding year. Fears about air travel following 9/11 and dealing with my husband's earlier prostate cancer had made me cancel a trip back to the UK. But in truth, I had not forgiven my father for introducing me to his longtime girlfriend half his age, and reading porn covertly at my mother's bedside during the time she was in a coma. So I had delayed seeing him until 2006, when I heard from my sister that his health had started to fail. Clearly, I am glad that I made those final trips back to see him, and wasn't entirely surprised to learn later that he was in hospital for a bladder infection. I saw him twice in hospital; the second visit was at his death bed in February 2007. Needless to say I had forgiven him in my heart for any transgressions during my visit the previous summer. What I saw was a very lonely old man, starved of human companionship, who sat hour after hour by his window, gazing at the people and the street below. We had a few nice dinners out together, and I bought him clean fresh bed linen. He was so happy to be taken care of by someone who loved him. By the time I made the first hospital visit, he had been diagnosed with Parkinson's and also with MRSA. The hospital was still trying to get him well enough to be discharged, but it was clearly an uphill battle. During my visits, I read the newspaper to him every day. I also had brought photos of the company's products and entertained him with stories about my business, and why we sell our products, and their contribution to health and a greener environment.

The next time I saw him he was dying. I was about to go to the Four Seasons hotel on a big family vacation in the Island of Nevis, leaving one Wednesday morning; I was all packed and ready to go. It was going to be a blast. Then late Tuesday afternoon the phone rang. It was my sister, who informed me that our father was dying. She had thought of not telling me, but had decided that she should give me the option of coming over. To me there was no choice to be made, and I dropped everything and got on the next plane to England. My father looked like a living skeleton, and it was shocking to behold. He was alert, but was fast losing the ability to speak. The nurse said it could be hours or days, she couldn't tell. I knew that my father had remained alive in order to say goodbye to me, and when we were finished, he would go. So I wrote a cheat sheet with a very long list of family memories, which I read aloud to him. He held my hand tightly, squeezing it hard and smiling the best he could. His gaze never left my face, except to turn to my sister when I referenced her. I was determined to give him a good death. Sometimes I broke down and just laid my head on the bed and wept, and he patted my head to comfort me. We both knew he was dying, and there was no denying it. After the second day, by about 10 p.m., I had run out of family memories to recall, and his favorite Gilbert and Sullivan songs to sing to him. I had been at the hospital for 12 hours and was exhausted; it was time to go home to sleep. I will never forget him turning to look at me as I was leaving his room, those blue eyes of his staring at me for the last time. The nurse said to me that she would see us in the morning, but I knew better. There was not going to be any tomorrow, and told her that he would die that night. He died four hours later. It was a good death. He was surrounded by love till the end, and that is all anyone can hope for—not to be alone and surrounded by love. Escorting someone to the end of their life is a truly sacred and privileged task.

His death hit me hard. I told my husband that one of the two men who had loved me unconditionally was now gone, and he was the only one I had left. Little did I know that he too would be leaving me soon. Meanwhile, in blissful ignorance, I made plans to sell our house in Newton and move into our summer home in Plymouth, where I thought Herman and I would be spending happy years together in retirement. My father's death was telling me in no uncertain terms that it was time to leave my business behind and enjoy my husband's company. As they say, the best laid plans went sadly astray.

My husband Herman was diagnosed with a brain tumor, Glioblastoma (GBM) on June 2nd, 2009, and he died on September 23, 2011. Becoming a caregiver to this proud and brilliant man, watching the beast of GBM slowly devour him, and then letting go of the man who made me happier than I have ever known in any other time of my life, was harder than I could ever had imagined. This time my anguish and sorrow seemed to know no depths. I still can hardly bear to look back, as there seems to be no point in reliving those agonizing years as a caregiver, during which I watched helplessly while he gradually lost all his physical and cognitive capacities. Brain cancer is a hideous disease, and for me as the spouse to watch its progression, was hell on earth. I was determined to make every day of his life count and make sure that there was joy in it. I fought GBM alongside him with everything I knew how to do, knowing all the while I would eventually lose the battle. It is fair to say that some days I hated my life, and to this day I hate brain cancer with a passion. Nobody can ever prepare you for the brutality of brain cancer in its final stages.

I will never forget the day he died and the days preceding it. He had fallen just one too many times—one of the hazards of GBM patients who are too proud to use a walker. Their lack of balance and short, mini seizures makes falling a constant hazard. For the last five weeks of his life, Herman was mostly flat on his back, healing from a slight but painful fracture. Each day I saw yet another cognitive function fall away and medication was the only way to keep hallucinations and delusions at bay. Slowly, and for him deeply humiliating, he lost control of his bodily functions. I would sit for hours on end massaging his arms and hands and trying to comfort him. He finally realized that the GBM beast was overtaking him, and when he asked me if he was dying, I told him yes. While I had given him my absolute best as a caregiver over the past 28 months, I was wracked with a sense of inadequacy. What more could I have done? I knew rationally that all I could have done was my best, but it always felt like it was not enough. I asked his forgiveness for my shortcomings.

He lay in a coma unresponsive for a week, but I never stopped sitting and holding his hand, softly talking to him. I knew he could hear me and when I went down late at night in my nightdress to wish him goodnight, I would kiss him and ask him to respond if he heard me. He always kissed me firmly back and I felt his love, perhaps more keenly than any other time in our lives. I knew he did not want to leave me. And then came the unmistakeable death rattle. On September 23, 2011, I stepped out of the room for no more than ten minutes just to grab a snack and then I heard a blood curdling scream from downstairs. I ran downstairs and said to the health aide: "What happened? I heard him scream." She replied that there had been no scream, but my husband had just passed away. I knew I had heard his soul leave his body and it was a cry out to me, one last time. I opened the patio doors and sat with his body quietly sobbing, until I knew that his spirit had exited the room. In death, all the pain and wrinkles had melted away, making him look 15 years younger. He was at peace, free from this deadly disease at last. I walked upstairs and sat in the silence and stillness of my house. The silence was welcome since, with hospice, health aides and the ever present visitors, I had had no privacy for weeks on end. So I sat in the stillness, trying to comprehend that now I was a widow, and the man who had given me the gift of unconditional love was now gone. Yet, because of the misery of his disease, there was also a curious sense of relief. We were now both free of this living hell.

Many months later, I was thinking about one of the things about which Herman had counseled me. His advice was to go on living without him and to find new love on this Earth, and he would wait for me in Heaven. As any widow knows, that is easier said than done. I was just picking up the pieces in my life; I even ventured out on a date or two, after the worst of my grieving was at least fading in intensity. Then my company suffered internal financial mismanagement, and my own cancer reared its ugly head.

I have had plenty of time during my own illness to contemplate what I have learned, and how I have changed since Herman's illness and death. The day he was diagnosed with brain cancer changed my life and who I am forever. I would like to think I am a better person for it all, wiser, kinder, and more compassionate. I do not sweat the small stuff, try not to complain, and treasure life in the moment. Perhaps that realization is the most profound of all; all you have are moments, and since your life can be taken from you without warning, make those moments count. Why am I telling you all of this? I think it is because I see too many people wasting their lives with bitterness and complaints. This saddens me because, if you open your eyes, there are daily miracles and so much to rejoice. That doesn't mean I do not miss my loved ones, especially my husband, whom I will carry forever in my heart. But my own life has been spared and I interpret it to mean that God has some other purpose for me in store. I just have to find it. And my need to find another special man in my life is growing as the end of my own cancer treatment draws near. I do not want to keep grieving for what and who I cannot have anymore. I want to have another man who lights up when I call out and say: "Honey, I'm home!" and rushes to greet me with a big kiss and a hug, and tells me how much he loves me. All the death and illness in my life has brought me tremendous love from my greater community, but my heart hungers for something more. When I eventually find it, I will treasure it like a rare jewel.

I was speaking to a friend this week—one of my drivers, Peter—on the way to Mass General. I remarked that I knew that the brunt of my cancer treatment was finally coming to an end this week. Contrary to what you might expect, I wasn't whooping and hollering with joy; my feelings were more of a vague realization that it will be soon time to rebuild my life. I didn't know whether the analogy of the butterfly emerging from the cocoon, or whether the phoenix rising from the ashes was more appropriate. He replied that the butterfly is predetermined in color, shape and species, but in my case, rising up from the ashes is more appropriate, for my exact shape in my new life is, as yet, undetermined. The deaths of my loved ones in recent years, financial shenanigans in my company, and my own illness have certainly reduced my life as I once knew it to ashes. It will never be the same, and I need to find its new shape—its shape is not predetermined. But what occurred to me is something that I have mentioned before. "You only have one life, so do not waste it." That has been my mantra for a long time. Now it has a new depth of meaning. The events in my own life in recent years have shown me that life as I know it can change in the blink of an eye. So to not relish even the teeniest, tiny joys that can be found in the present, every day, is wasting life. And one thing is certain, life does not go on forever. Sooner or later death will take us all.

Lesson learned: You have only one life, do not waste it. This answer to my purpose has been under my nose for a long time. Finally, I could see it clearly at last.

RADIATION FINISH LINE
October 17th, 2014

I got off the radiation table for the last time this morning with tears in my eyes. This 7-week daily ordeal is now over. You might think that I should be dancing with joy; no, it was deep emotional relief. I have finally got to the end of this part of my treatment. I feel very quiet and introspective, letting the reality sink in that the worst is over, after nine straight grueling months. It will be time to start rebuilding my life soon. My health, my business, and eventually a new partner in my life. But for right now, I dwell in the silence.

JANE, MY SUCCESSFUL TWIN
October 18th, 2014

The rules for writing a "My Successful Twin" essay are the following: my twin, as opposed to me and all my usual thoughts of "Why not?" can have the life she wants without restriction. It is a visioning exercise where a clear message is sent out to the universe and, over time, you will then see how your life and your successful twin actually become one. I used to give this exercise to participants in my personal growth courses back some 20 or moreyears ago. The first time I wrote "My Successful Twin" for myself and read it to Herman shortly after I met him, he asked whether I had written the part about my love life after I had met him, because the details were uncannily synchronistic. I smiled. My Successful Twin had been written some five years previously. I used to take my essay out and review it every year, as a reminder of how I wanted my life to turn out, and eventually, slowly and imperceptibly, my life and that of my twin became one.

Her Purpose For Life

Jane's life has had a common theme throughout. It has always been about educating, supporting, and inspiring others around mental and physical health issues. At different times, that purpose for her life has found different expressions and manifestations, but each time she has found a wider audience for her wisdom and the causes about which she is passionate.

Her Health

Jane enjoys excellent health, which she treasures deeply and does not take for granted, after recovering from her breast cancer a few years earlier. This is now, thankfully, safely behind her and she is cancer free. So Jane respects her body; has lost weight and eats clean, healthy food; takes long walks in nature; and practices regularly on her pilates machine. She walks easily, with a long loping stride, and enjoys the vitality that comes with her supple body. After her illness a few years back, Jane has devised a life for herself that is far less stressful than when she was managing a struggling business. She has time for reflection and to enjoy her friends, her new husband, her cats and the beauty of the natural world. She sleeps well and is at peace with herself and life.

Where She Lives

Jane bases herself in a beautiful golf planned community in Plymouth, MA, but she also spends a few months in the winter out of MA in a warmer climate. While she is by nature a homebody, who loves her home and garden, Jane also "lives" out there in the world, as she sometimes travels far and wide in order to bring her message to the wider community.

What She Does For Recreation

Jane loves to be outdoors, either walking, golfing, traveling, gardening, or taking photographs of nature. It is when she is enjoying the beauty of the outdoor world that she is at her most peaceful. But she also enjoys indoor pursuits, whether reading, playing bridge, seeing the occasional good movie and, of course, dining with friends. She is especially proud that, after a hiatus of over ten years, she has resumed playing indoor tennis.

What She Does For Work

Jane sold her company a few years ago. It was sold to a larger company who were able to take "her baby" and grow it. While Jane did not sell her company at the peak of its value, nevertheless she made enough money for a very comfortable, if not ostentatious lifestyle. She had been very proud of her company, which she had built up over 15 years, and stayed with it a few years after the sale to help it turnaround and grow again. But she recognized, after her illness, that it would be eventually time for a change. Time to live a less stressful life if she didn't want her cancer to return, and one that was expressive of her current passions and expressions in the healthcare field. She wrote a book during her recovery, in which she used her illness as a springboard for deep reflection for the secrets to having a happy life, despite adversity. She knows only too well, from events in her own life, that one's time on earth is finite, and it distresses her to see so many people, as she sees it, "wasting life" by being unhappy and sweating the small stuff. Jane published her book through Amazon and other channels and, much to her surprise, it has become a runaway bestseller, inspiring hundreds of thousands of people all over the world, approaching one million e-copies sold. The book was a launching platform for resuming work that she loved as an inspirational speaker, which she had done some 20 plus years previously. Jane maintains an ongoing blog and Facebook page, which has many hundreds of thousands of followers. She is in high demand as a speaker, as her audiences love her British accent, her wit and raw honesty, and stories about her own life.

Her Friends

Jane has a very wide circle of friends who are attracted to her loving, giving, and optimistic energy. People like to be around her. Friends from all around the world come to visit her and she, likewise, can often be seen getting on a plane to see them. She feels blessed to have so many wonderful friends, many of whom supported her through her cancer journey. Other friends have come into her life more recently, after hearing her at one of her speaking engagements. Jane never feels isolated.

Her Love Life

After being a caregiver to her late husband, who suffered from a terminal illness some years ago, Jane is now very happily remarried to a man, Bill, whom she loves deeply. He doesn't wish her late husband any ill will, but is very thankful to have the opportunity to have Jane in his life. He absolutely adores her, and respects what she is doing with her life in her so called "retirement years." He never ceases to tell her how much he loves her, and how lucky he feels that she is in his life. He hugs her constantly, and they both love the intimacy of just curling up with each other in bed. Jane and Bill are never bored with each other's company. They love having long philosophical and political discussions, as well as exchanging their news of the day over the dinner table. They often prepare their meals together, as they both like cooking. Bill, like Jane, spends a good deal of his time contributing to the lives of others, so they both have a purpose for living that is outside themselves. Bill and Jane share many interests in common, making good companions and always have enough time to play together. Bill and Jane both realize that life is finite, so in their relationship they make every effort to bring joy, kindness and caring into the other's life through their partnership. Their love is evident, as they each light up when the other walks into the room. Jane's happiness at home allows her to go out and make her contribution to the rest of the world. The security of her relationship on the home front is very important to her.

PostScript

So there we have it. It is Jane's life that I want. It is my prayer, my wish, and my hope.

Lesson learned: If you do not begin to dream you will never have what you want. So start dreaming! I will never give up my dreams.

IT IS NOT OVER YET
October 22nd, 2014

Yesterday in hospital was exhausting and dispiriting. Apart from a raft of relatively minor symptoms, in the grand scheme of things, I have a bad case of post-radiation fatigue; apparently my oncologist is not surprised that it is getting worse before it gets better. It is a well documented post reaction to radiation. It is quite extraordinary; all I do is sleep and graze on an occasional snack. I had 15 hours of sleep last night, and I think I will be going back to nap soon after breakfast.

Due to potential complications with the cancer having spread to the chest wall, I will not get a final "cancer free" blessing and prognosis till May 2015, when scans of all parts of my body are repeated and infusions complete. The journey is far from over yet.

My oncologist says that this intense phase will last another couple of weeks, but by Thanksgiving I will feel closer to normal.

Lesson learned: The road to success will be strewn with setbacks. Accept them, but know they all move you closer to your goals.

DIGGING FOR MIRACLES
October 25th, 2014

Sometimes, when one is in a pity party kind of funk, it is easy to be oblivious to the daily miracles. You just want to toss them to one side and sulk. While this not my normal Modus Operandi, the news that the definitive blessing for my cancer-free declaration will not be until next May, plus the unwarned worsening post-radiation fatigue, threw me for a loop. To begin with, I did nothing but mope and sleep, and I truly mean nothing. I just crawled under a rock, refused all social invitations, and went to sleep. This butterfly was firmly zipped up in her cocoon.

But then I look back on the week, and I am now giving myself a little pep talk. Bunches of fall flowers came from Rose and Debbie, and Jan came by for an unexpected visit, complete with goodies, providing sympathetic companionship when I needed it. Sandy dashed in and out to change the cat litter and clean up the remnants of "cat tummy." Lovely caring emails came from friends like Pat, when I was just too tired to get into a car and visit anyone.

Other friends provided a listening ear when I needed it. Everyone told me to be patient; the fatigue would be over soon, and then I could start healing.

My goodness, I can hardly wait! I tried putting on a bra today, which was an exercise in futility. One side is still huge, hard, and swollen. I just have to accept this. I have zero control over how long it will take to go down in size. But there's one thing I do have control over: the color of my hair. You might think I would be rejoicing that there is a little covering on my formerly bald pate, but quite frankly I had become sick of seeing a grey headed, almost bald apparition every day in the mirror. I cannot control the incredibly slow rate of growth of my hair, but my hair got a temporary color rinse today, so the grey wouldn't be poking out of my wig at the sides. I smiled at the woman in the mirror; she didn't look so old and haggard anymore. I am also pleased today that the self restraint I showed with my eating while Jon was not here has paid off with weight loss this week. I am 5 pounds heavier than I was when I started chemotherapy in February, and was stable until the last couple of months, when I celebrated the return of my tastebuds with enthusiastic and gay abandon. Thankfully, that phase is over and I lost just a little weight this week.

By some miracle I realized as I woke up today that the worst of the storm was passing. My sleep was down to ten hours last night and I woke up at 8 a.m. I have errands to do and I can see myself getting dressed and actually getting them done. This is progress.

Lesson learned: Seek and ye shall find—the miracles are always there. I seem to have to keep relearning this, as well as exercising patience in my health recovery.

THE BUSINESS DEBACLE
October 28th, 2014

I do not write much about my business and its problems achieving its profitability goals, yet all during this year it has remained a huge stress in my life. It has been the reason that Jon comes in here valiantly week after week to try to shift the culture and focus on achieving results. It is also my innermost conviction that I need to reduce the stress in my life if I am ever to have a chance of cancer not returning. For this reason I have made the decision to put my company up for sale in 2015.

After February 2013, and our discovery that my CFO was giving me fairy stories as to rosy non-existent profits, it occurred to me that if theft was not going on, in some ways, this was bad news. With straight theft, after I had emptied my savings to cover losses, we could quickly return to profitability. But we did not. Losses continued to mount, despite massive efforts to improve processes. But the core of the problem continued to elude me. How could we be generating so many millions of top line sales just to produce losses? I confess I was baffled.

In January 2014, Jon started as an adviser to my company with pretty much a free hand to effect change; he then volunteered to step up his involvement in August 2014 so I could concentrate on my health and selling the company. Since then we seem to be uncovering the real sources of our problems. I have given him complete control and he is acting president. While we discuss things over the dinner table, and some of his interventions have caused me to take a very sharp intake of breath, for the most part I have not interfered. Maybe I felt too sick and weary all this year to debate the issues with him. However, a good part of me has just kept the faith that he would have the persistence and courage to tackle the ways we habitually did business, where I felt I had not been able to intervene effectively. I have been able on occasion to point him in the right direction, or even lend an intelligent remark here and there. But I have not interfered pretty much all year; my way of managing the company appears to not be what the company needs right now. That saddens me, as I used to think of myself as a pretty good manager.

So I have watched and waited. Sometimes, transferring people from certain jobs and reassigning them to other positions in the company seemed like a draconian intervention. Then bit by bit, the root causes for our problems was uncovered. Each revelation, as Jon reported to me, has made me frustrated, sick and angry. Could it really be that I had been fobbed off with incomplete data and analysis by those unwilling to carry out quality control on their own work? Had I backed away where I should have been more insistent? If so, it is a character flaw. As Jon has intervened systematically in each area of the company—finance, sales, customer service, operations, and then the giant offender of them all, marketing—I am confronted with his assertion that the wastage was of mind boggling proportions. The grand total of wastage amounted to seven figures in value. No wonder staff had not received a raise in years, my own salary was slashed, and my retirement savings emptied, leaving a company that had been worth a tidy sum now of dubious, if any, value. I confess that my confidence in myself as a business person has been deeply shaken. It would appear that people whom I had trusted had let me down. Worse still, I have let myself down, and have put the entire company at risk, along with the livelihoods of people I care about. Is this all really true? I confess I am struggling with it all.

The reality of what has been happening is barely sinking in. The good news is, according to Jon, apparently I own a basically sound company. The bad news is it has been very badly managed. And the buck always stops on the CEO's desk. Many people have said that if my husband had not contracted brain cancer, then none of this would have happened to my company. I cannot tell you whether that is true or not.

What I can tell you is that I am proud of the company and its contribution to transforming our customers' health. I agree with Jon that we need to deeply examine the ways we conduct our business, and do a better job at using all avenues to communicate to our customers that we genuinely care about their health.

But I am confused. I wish my brain was working better. There is something in all this that doesn't quite make sense, and I do not have the concentration to figure it out.

THE MELON
October 29th, 2014

Two nights ago, before I went to bed, I stared at myself in the mirror. My left breast was huge, hard, and swollen, much more so than usual, well on the way to being the size of a small melon. I was horrified. I soon discovered on the Internet that there is something called "breast lymphedema." I only knew about arm lymphedema. Maybe that's what I had. Advice came from MGH swiftly. A nurse told me on the phone that I needed to get a special sports bra from a store that specializes in helping breast cancer patients. In the meantime, before I accomplish that task tomorrow, I am back to wearing a surgical vest, which of course also compresses me. It is not a very comfortable garment, to say the least. I will even need to wear the new bra overnight, at least for the time being.

But the good news is, although my energy is very limited, I have been able to pick up the phone and do a few very basic chores. My concentration for anything work related is almost non-existent, but nonetheless, I can feel my brain awakening very slowly. That is really good news. I just wish I could understand more clearly what is happening at my company—some of what Jon tells me about what he is doing, and why, is currently beyond my comprehension. However, even some occasional bouts of nausea or pains in my breast pale compared to my delight that this immense wall of fatigue seems to be crumbling at last. And then my brain will surely clear itself.

BREAST BURST
November 12th, 2014

The sports bra did not work, in fact it was a resounding failure. Not to go into too much detail about it, my left breast clearly decided that it had enough of swelling to the size of a cantaloupe. So it found the natural way out, through my nipple, and gave me the shock of my life as I found myself in a very damp pool after a Saturday afternoon nap. This spontaneous leaking continued for the next few days. The leaking was sufficient to go through two layers of towels onto my bed sheets. I must have lost at least 8-12 oz of fluid. Of course, like bursting a boil, I actually felt a bit better for it. But this constant leaking and refilling clearly is no way to conduct a life, and I knew it was a serious side effect, so again I contacted MGH. They summoned me in quickly for a physical examination.

It was immediately decided, after an ultrasound viewing last Wednesday, that I had a seroma, which is liquid filling the cavity after an operation. I do not have lymphodemia. So much for self diagnosis! The ultrasound team exclaimed, "Goodness, we have never seen anything like this before. You have a gigantic accumulation of fluid on the breast." I was rushed into ultrasound guided surgery. The senior doctor needed to take over, as my breast was not being cooperative and she needed to use a bigger needle to aspirate. With great persistence and skill she took out over 500cc of fluid, which is over a pint. My surgeon, Dr Hughes, warned me that my breast might refill before I saw him again on Monday. Indeed it did, so on Monday Dr Hughes tried to aspirate and managed to take out 30cc, but there was clearly much more to come out, so I need another ultrasound guided aspiration. Day surgery is scheduled this coming Friday with the same aspiration specialist as before. Dr Hughes has warned me that, in his experience, this approach would not solve the problem permanently and he would need to open me up again for surgery to insert drains. Now instead of wearing the surgical vest in the daytime, as I had been doing for the last four months, I have to wear it 24 hours a day.

Quite frankly, I found this news exceptionally discouraging. Just as I was experiencing some relief from the pain in my swollen breast, and my energy post radiation was picking up little by little, there is yet another setback. I was even starting to envisage a new life; now I am feeling like a pin cushion, and there is no end in sight.

I am just taking a deep breath and taking it one day at a time again. It takes great resolve not to worry about having to endure another surgery, or not driving again for weeks post-surgery, and being a one-armed bandit again. I confess it does prey on my mind. How could it not?

HERE WE GO AGAIN
November 20th, 2014

Last Friday, I lay on the operating table, all drenched with iodine, waiting for the doctor to do an ultrasound guided aspiration. As I lay there, before she began, I heard her tell the junior doctor in assistance to look at the ultrasound screen. She pointed out to him the signs that my body was trying to heal itself from the radiation trauma, but that with all the new blood vessels that had recently appeared, one teeny wrong move on her part and a blood vessel could burst. I could keep silent no longer, and told her that her comments were making me very nervous. She replied that she had decided it was too dangerous to do the aspiration. If she burst a blood vessel I would be in emergency surgery within the hour, and it would be even worse if a blood vessel burst after I returned home. This gave me chills. She went and paged my surgeon, Dr Hughes, who said he wanted to see me and discuss the situation early the following week.

The ultrasound doctor gave me what I thought at the time was excellent advice. She advised that seromas often get reabsorbed into the body over many months, and if I could stand the pain, and could see that each week my breast was gradually getting smaller, then the slow route held less risks for me. She reminded me that surgery would be yet another trauma to my body and would cause a new inflammation from which my body needed to heal. She also warned me that I might have to bear the inconvenience and pain of not just one but maybe several inconveniently situated drains. She said that the point of "I cannot stand this any longer" was an individual decision. It could be that bursting through again via the nipple may prove to be my breaking point—that was her guess. She reminded me that the nipple discharge was nature's way of trying to handle the problem.

It sounded like good advice, but I had found the afternoon very stressful, and for the first time as Debbie drove me home, and later that evening when I was dining with Rose, I found myself with tears rolling down my face. I missed my husband. Where was he when I needed him to take care of me? The only thing I can say is, thank goodness for friends who can pick me up off the ground when I'm in a puddle.

So I watched and waited over the weekend, hoping that my body was going to be strong enough to heal itself and the swelling start to subside. Unfortunately, I could see over the next four days that my breast was getting relentlessly larger and the discomfort increasing. I was filled with many questions prior to the appointment with my surgeon, and the questions swirled around in my brain. I had a sneaking suspicion that surgery would be inevitable, but would it cure the problem? What are the risks? How long would the recovery be this time? These questions and more plagued me.

So I had the discussion with Dr Hughes, accompanied by my friend Debbie, who had a list of questions to ask him when my mind would go predictably blank.

My seroma has been caused by surgery and pushing the edges of a lumpectomy. It would not have happened with a complete mastectomy. We are all hoping that the pain will subside and the swelling will recede, even if only by minuscule amounts each week. That way I can avoid surgery. However, if it keeps swelling this rapidly and eventually bursts, then surgical intervention will be necessary. The good news is that only one drain would be involved. But, like any surgery, it will take time to heal, although the operation will obviously not be as extensive as before. The bad news is there is no guarantee that it will solve the problem, and quite naturally my surgeon is reluctant to do a complete mastectomy to resolve a seroma. Therefore, surgery is tentatively scheduled for December 12th, and everyone hopes that in the end, it will get canceled.

In the meantime, I will try to return my life to as normal as possible; all the while my breast ominously and stubbornly continues to swell.

SANDY
November 24th, 2014

Sandy has been a ministering angel to me all year.

In the couple of years following Herman's death, I used to take a cooked dinner to her on a weekend night, while she looked after her husband with Alzheimer's, and waited for that last minute drive-by B&B guest to call. She knew and loved my husband, so she understood in those early months when tears would rush to my eyes. We both knew what it was like to care for someone whose brain is not functioning correctly, and the pain involved in watching that degradation of the brain. She used to say that I was her entire social life, and my dinners were incredibly welcome and appreciated. For many, there are very few people in their lives with whom they can share their innermost feelings without fear of judgment. Sandy has been one of them for me.

During 2014, the nature of our relationship changed because of my illness. Whenever I could drive a car, I would visit at her B&B on a lonely weekend night, and she would cook me dinner, always listening carefully to what I could or could not eat, even in the depths of my chemotherapy. In fact, because I was so terrified of chemo, she had me as her house guest for the few days following my first two rounds of infusions. Every time this year when I have been over at her house, she has given me a bead-filled hand warmer, and has been a treasure trove of practical advice on how to deal with all the irritating side effects of my treatment. She constantly comforted me when I was nearing despair, or when my body was in agony. I looked forward to our "good night, dear friend" nightly texts. There have also been times, knowing how sick I was, that she would jump in her car and change my bed sheets, empty the dishwasher, clean up cat puke and change the kitty litter, just flying in and out during her busy day.

This year we have shared our terror of our ailing finances. Hers derived from the conflict between being a caregiver, and the responsibilities of being an inn keeper. Mine came from an unprofitable company devastating my retirement savings. We both reached a point, for different reasons, where we decided to sell our businesses, recognizing we could not do it all. We both had other priorities in our lives. Mine was my own health. Hers was the health of her husband.

But it was with profound sadness that I learned this last weekend that she had sold the house and business and was moving to Texas, where property prices are cheaper. What's more, she would be leaving at the turn of the year. This Thanksgiving will be the last that I spend with her. There will be no more Saturdays filling the lonely nights of a widow, discussing my week with someone who truly loved me. I have girlfriends all over the country, and enjoy their company when my health permits, even going to visit them. But it will not be the same. It never is, and when I came home after learning this news, I had tears in my eyes.

I applaud Sandy for taking those first steps towards the new chapter in her life, because we have always encouraged each other to keep moving forward. And when she said that I was the only reason she had considered staying in Massachusetts, I knew she meant it. I also know that Texas has some other benefits for her, since she will be closer to family. But it doesn't change the fact that her leaving will be a huge loss in my life. She is an angel and I love her deeply. Friends do not come better than Sandy. She is one of a kind.

SANDY: A FAREWELL

You were there to comfort me,
And hold my shaking hand.
You gave me courage
When despair came knocking on the door.
You soothed my troubled spirit
When I was so confused.
You told me a new life would come
When I could hardly see.

A truer friend I would not want.
And now, you are leaving me.
I say farewell
And wish you BonVoyage
As your life will start anew.
But when all is said and done
I will truly miss you.

Mercia Tapping

BE THANKFUL
Thanksgiving, November 27th, 2014

Like many widows, the reality of my marital status hits particularly hard at holiday times, and to be truthful, I am thankful when the holidays are over and the normal rhythm of life can return. Yet as I write this, I know how strange it may sound. Life has been far from normal for me this year, and will never be the same. Yet, I am alive at the end of it and I am beginning to get a sneak peek of just maybe what my life could be like. I spent Thanksgiving at Sandy's. It was bittersweet, since I know it will be our last together. But it was a happy afternoon with delicious food and good friends.

A male friend of mine recently predicted that as my health improves the increased loneliness and new free time at weekends will drive me once again to be open to a romantic partner. He reminded me how much energy I had before my illness began, and how I had enjoyed a very busy social life. He was sweet enough to say that I had a very big and open heart, and without a doubt I would find someone who will appreciate me for who I am. His confidence in me made me smile.

I find I am increasingly looking forward to the new chapter in my life as my health improves and energy slowly returns.

ROUTE 3 THANKSGIVING
November 27th, 2014

The highway says "Enter Here" and then "No Turns"
As the Plymouth Highway stretches out beyond,
But to where? The destination is your choice.
Our pilgrim fathers fought for their truth, their freedom,
And for their voices to be heard.
To your own self be true.
Let your voice ring out, with courage and conviction,
Like the pilgrims of yesteryear,
Giving thanks in this new land
For life to be lived anew.

Mercia Tapping

A MIRACLE IN THE MAKING?
November 28th, 2014

Over the past couple of days, I have been feeling the tissue in my breast with a growing sense of incredulity. The tissue, which has been immoveable and as rigid as a piece of granite for weeks, is showing some microscopic signs of being "squishy" again around the edges. This I would take to mean that the seroma fluid might actually be re-absorbing into my body. Amazingly enough, it could indicate that my body might be healing itself! If that is happening and I might actually avoid another surgery, I will really feel incredibly blessed. This would be my Thanksgiving miracle! To me it would signify that God thinks I have suffered enough, and it is time for me to share my life lessons learned with the greater community.

But I do not have confidence in my own observations. One moment I think I see improvement; certainly my breast size seems to have stabilized and is less painful. But as for any size decrease? Is it wishful thinking? I honestly do not know.

FAT CHANCE
December 3rd, 2014

My body has clearly spoken. I get a modest amount of temporary relief after a massage, which stimulates the lymphatic system, but the reality is that my breast is relentlessly increasing in size. I will be lucky if it doesn't burst again before December 12th, which is the date of the surgery. I have to look at this as a temporary setback, otherwise it's all too depressing.

Mentally and physically, I have been gradually getting stronger each week. My recovery is far slower than I anticipated, but I cannot control this, so I have stopped fretting about how slow it all seems. Emotionally, I am simply ready to move to the next phase of my life: regain my health and fitness, publish this book, let people know I am available for speaking engagements, sell my business, and eventually find a new romantic partner. It is time to rise up again from my sickbed, and lead a more public life again in 2015. Surgery will just have to be a temporary blip on the horizon.

THE YEAR IS COMING TO A CLOSE
December 15th, 2014

I am sitting at home recuperating after my surgery last Friday, the goal of which is to drain the seroma fluid from my breast. Yes, I have a drain and my breast is sore, but quite frankly, compared to what I have been through, this is a temporary bump in the road and has not affected my brain. Jon kindly took me to surgery at 4:15 a.m. and stayed over this past weekend to keep an eye on me. It is very reassuring to have someone else in the house in case of emergencies. Also, even though I cannot drive, we still have a set of wheels in residence.

Since my surgeon told me to do nothing physical for a few days, I am busying myself with finishing this book, and the launch of my new blog and Facebook page, which will carry on where this book leaves off.

But the best thing is I am truly looking forward to life again. I will be enjoying going back to work at my company and actively contributing in areas where I can be useful. I like the challenges and assisting my staff in solving problems. It is delightful to find my brain is returning rapidly. Also, while my company has been sailing pretty close to the wind financially, nevertheless I still have confidence that, with Jon at the helm uncovering all the sources of unprofitability, we have an excellent fighting chance of turning the ship around and becoming profitable again. I confess that I do not fully understand Jon's turn-around strategy, but I am keeping the faith. To return the company to profitability would be a huge contribution to my life, as any entrepreneur would want to end on an up note, with their head held high, and not with their tail between their legs.

My treatment for breast cancer is not entirely over. In the New Year I still have to face hormone therapy and infusion of antibodies every three weeks till May 2015. But the worst of the breast cancer treatment marathon is over, which is an enormous relief. In case you are interested, I am now six months out from chemotherapy and I have a thick head of hair, wavy, but all of an inch plus long. Almost to the length where I could sport it au natural. Friends think it's cute, but I am far from convinced. I still miss my longer hair and wear a wig in public.

But as I look out into 2015, I can envisage myself being out on the golf course once more and being far more sociable again. I have really been a social recluse throughout 2014 and that is not my normal Modus Operandi. I will resume a life that includes being outdoors, speaking engagements, writing on topics about which I feel passionate, as well as making sure our customers at AllergyBuyersClub.com realize that we truly care about their health. My life will be busy and full. Romance would be the icing on the cake but not necessary for me to enjoy life once more.

MY SPIRITUAL LIFE REVISITED
December 19th, 2014

I have always seen myself as a spiritual person in as much as I have tried to live by the golden rule, but have had no formal religious affiliation since leaving my Catholic high school. I have never considered myself an atheist, but certainly would admit to being an agnostic for a good deal of my adult life. However, things have changed in the last few years, and despite my former skepticism about a form of existence beyond life on Earth, I am now convinced that God and Heaven do exist.

A week after Herman died, I had my first and complimentary reiki session with a woman whom I had not met before. I had been disturbed by a sense of Herman's spirit around me all week, and hearing voices in my head. In desperation, the night before the reiki session, I had shouted out into the emptiness of the house, "If you are for real, show me a sign that I cannot argue with!" I thought I was losing my marbles. The reiki session was a pleasant enough relaxing experience, and I closed my eyes and listened to the music. When the 15-minute session was over, I asked the therapist whether she sensed anything about me.

She replied, "I sense that you are a bit stuck in moving forward in some areas of your life."

I was hardly impressed, most people are a bit stuck somewhere, and after all I had only been widowed a week. I then asked, "Did you sense anything else?"

She hesitated and replied, "There is something, I don't know what it means, but I feel I am supposed to give you a message, maybe it will make sense to you."

She piqued my curiosity. "Please go ahead," I said.

"I have been told to give you a marshmallow. Does that make any sense?"

Indeed it did. I sat bolt upright with tears springing to my eyes. Marshmallow was the name of my favorite, and now deceased, Siamese cat. If my husband was ever going to get my attention, it would be through one of my cats. It was in that moment that I had a complete revelation; Heaven was indeed for real and my husband was watching over me. It was one of those seminal moments in life that you remember forever.

Over the past three or more years, Herman has reminded me of the spirit world numerous times, and each time it has left me with tears streaming down my face. On the one hand, it is comforting to be certain of an existence beyond that which we know on Earth, but it is also like stretching your hand out to something you are close to physically touching, but still eludes you. Any widow will tell you they only wish they could touch and hear their spouse just one more time. With the passing of the years after Herman's death, I came to accept that he was like a big guardian angel, stepping in to help me when I needed it most.

But my relationship with God was still a puzzle. I was far less skeptical, but I was far from being a believer. I was driving along one day, pondering why I was still here on Earth, and why, although I had cancer, my life had been spared. I turned my eyes to Heaven and asked Herman to give me the answers and guidance. By this time, I was used to having conversations with Herman, and believed in their validity. However, I was very surprised when another, completely different voice came through who identified itself as God. And the message was clear: I was being saved because I was worth it and I still had a job to do on Earth. You might think I would be ecstatic at having such an experience. No, I told the voice rather crossly, if I now told people I was talking to God, they might think I was losing my mind. And I told the voice firmly, we aren't going to do this too often. I did eventually recount this experience to Sandy. She told me that I was very blessed, that there were people who had prayed all their lives to hear the voice of God directly without success. And then there was me, hearing it unbidden.

It is still one of those experiences that I find inexplicable and uncomfortable, but I now fully acknowledge the existence of the Divine; its intervention in our lives and, moreover, that there is a higher purpose for events to which I might not be privy in the present. I have not undergone some cataclysmic formal religious conversion, but my spiritual life has been undergoing some profound changes. Strangely enough, I have far more of an inner sense of peace than at any time of my life, and for that I am grateful.

WRITING THIS BOOK

December 21st, 2014

I wrote this book for several reasons.

Firstly, by keeping journal entries of what was undoubtedly one of the worst years of my life, I sought to heal myself by writing not only about the pain, but also the miracles that occurred along the way. Both pain and miracles occurred in abundance. Perhaps the most extraordinary thing of all was the love and compassion shown to me by friends, as well as by perfect strangers.

Secondly, I sought to find my voice, and by that I meant the ability to write and speak on subjects about which I am passionate. I have always written and spoken from the heart, and after my husband's death, my world was flat and muted. I am finding my voice again and I have an increasing clarity of purpose for this next phase of my life. That clarity both brings me peace and a sense of excitement about the future.

Thirdly, it was my intention when starting this book that it would somehow inspire others who have to travel a similar path to mine in the future. It is an autobiographical tale of rising up with courage to face incredible adversity and tragedy, and the eventual triumph of the human spirit. We all need to be reminded of that. I intend to carry my message of "Only One Life: Don't Waste It," not only through this book, but through speaking engagements, a blog, and Facebook page. This message will be the final legacy of my life for as long as God chooses to keep me on this planet.

MY LIFE HAS BEEN TURNED UPSIDE DOWN
January 18th, 2015

Usually, one begins a New Year full of optimism, hope, and good reso-
lutions. Indeed, I was glad down to the tips of my toes to see the end of
2014. It will forever in my head be dubbed my "cancer year." I had every
reason to be optimistic. While Jon Rivers had said it would be a close
call, nevertheless he exuded confidence in his turnaround strategy for
my company. He promised substantial profits and surplus cash flow by
the turn of the year. While I had placed my trust in him and he was the
acting president, I had an increasing sense of unease. As my brain was
slowly waking up after radiation, I asked Jon questions when he came
home at night. Some things were just not adding up in my mind.

If I look back on it now, I could see that there was a palpable shift in
Jon's attitude and behavior towards me, dating back to the end of the
summer or even earlier. But being sick as I was, and with a compromised
brain, I brushed those observations and feelings to one side, although
I did share my concerns with a couple of close girlfriends. I began to
feel that I was not welcome over the threshold of my own company,
and expressed the same to Jon. I told him that since I was recovering
from radiation, I needed to be around more at our workplace, but not
with the intention of interfering with his work as acting president. I felt
if I was to sell the company in early 2015, I needed to understand what
was going on in every corner of the company. If I did not understand
how my company was operating and how Jon was brilliantly turning it
around, I would not be able to answer the probing questions of interested buyers. I did not want to appear like the washed-up, out of touch
founder who should be put out to pasture as soon as possible.

My sister Susan, who is a judge in England, had always said that if
Jon Rivers ever thought he would not be able to turn around my company, that he would abruptly resign, blame it all on me, and I would
never see him again. Her reasoning was he would never be able to
admit or own any failure and live with that failure on his record. I
remember at the time being rather taken aback by her assessment and

potential omen, and said of course I hoped it would never come to that. She proved to be right in a way that I would never have predicted. I trusted Jon and deemed him as close a friend as anybody could be to someone who was not their spouse. Except for being lovers, in all other ways we could not have been closer. My whole world was filtered through his eyes. Except for a couple of close girlfriends, he was my window to the world.

On Monday, December 22nd, Jon abruptly resigned via Skype after he had left Boston the previous Friday. He was savage in his criticism of me and as cold as ice. I was stunned and remembered my sister's predictions. It was only ten days after my last surgery on December 12th. I staggered into work, although I was not cleared to drive. I just did what I needed to do. I was astonished and very dismayed at what I found after I went around the company asking my staff questions. There was much that was very different from what I had been given to believe. It was hard to reconcile those two disparate realities, and the new reality is a nightmare. No wonder Jon had bailed out. There was no pot of gold at the end of the rainbow for him. There was only one option left that had any salvageable potential, and that was to conduct an accelerated and emergency sale of the company. It was clear that the company would not survive without a significant and immediate injection of funds.

My staff have rallied around. They are so relieved to see me back at the helm, but they are very worried. And quite understandably so. It has been painful to realize how frightened, demoralized, and browbeaten they were by Jon. My brain and energy level improves each day, but 12-hour days and an excruciating level of stress leave me beyond exhausted. I try as much as possible to discipline my brain not to obsess about business issues in the middle of the night. And I wake up to the new nightmare reality each day. I am fighting hard for the survival of my company, its vision, my employees, and to do the right thing by our customers and vendors to whom we owe money. I do not have time to mourn the loss of Jon Rivers in my life or even to be angry with him. I just have to believe that he resigned in the nick of time and it is only me, the company's founder, that can save the company. I have to keep that faith.

I also believe, and this is a belief not universally shared by others, that Jon Rivers began 2014 with the purest of intentions; namely to help a friend in need and turn around her company while she battled breast cancer. I cannot doubt the motives of a man who tried hard to tempt my appetite or make me laugh when I was going through chemotherapy, or got up at 3 a.m. to take me to surgery. We had so many intimate, sweet, and precious moments when my world was full of pain and my brain was shot to pieces. He was my hero, Heaven sent to rescue me. I felt very blessed. I trusted Jon implicitly, even while often I had struggled to understand his business advice. But somewhere along the line, slowly and almost imperceptibly at first, something went terribly wrong, and a darker side to his personality emerged. I turned a blind eye. I tried to brush it off at first as lapses due to the stress of the work challenges at hand. Certainly, I think turning around my company was just beyond his capability and industry experience, and he was too arrogant to take advice. I knew that anyone who specializes in turnarounds has to be pretty hard nosed and rational about what they see and advise. But in the end I, like many of my staff, felt demeaned, disparaged, and did not appreciate his bullying behavior. Jon held a big piece of my heart during 2014, and I bear him no ill will or anger, despite my being very significantly financially poorer at the end of his tenure at the business. It will take time for me to put the two years that I knew him into perspective. I still care for him at some level, and appreciate what he set out to do for me, despite the failed outcome. I think his behavior was reflective of a man who did not want to fail, but knew that his policies were not working. His barking at everyone was just an inner manifestation of his internal stress and dawning realization that he was the captain of an impending train wreck. I am not the kind of person who can switch off caring feelings for anyone overnight, but it is best if I cease communication with him. No good can come of it, since he was intent on rewriting history to avoid confronting failure and his share of the responsibility for the result. I just have sadness that our friendship, which I had always held to be so very special, ended on such a sour note.

But any thoughts about Jon will have to wait, as I have a company to run and hopefully to sell to an appropriate buyer. The situation at work could not be more bleak. At least I tell myself that I only have a few weeks left of an open drain in my breast, and my brain continues to sharpen daily. But each day when I wake up, I have to find the courage to keep on going, to persist where others would have given up and raised the white flag. I am beyond exhausted. I have always known that selling a company is stressful, but selling under these circumstances is particularly hard. I am, quite frankly, terrified that I will not have enough money to live, even on a vastly reduced budget.

SISTERLY ADVICE
January 25th, 2015

I was recounting my tale of woe to my sister in England during our weekly Sunday Facetime call. I expressed my dismay at my inability to face the truth of what was happening at my company during 2014, despite a nagging little voice in the back of my head. Was it my caring and admiration for Jon, or my illness with cancer that had made me so blind? My faith in my otherwise historically sound judgment in life had been sorely shaken. Would I be ever able to trust myself again, especially in my judgment of men? I know that eventually I want to spend my life in a relationship with another man again, but would my emotions cloud my judgment? My sister's advice and perspective was swift but clear.

What she said was in 2014 there was a unique confluence of the three main rivers in my life: my health, my work, and my heart. Those three rivers got inextricably intertwined, and the result was very muddy waters, with each river being dependent on the other. She said it was highly unlikely that those exact circumstances would ever exist again in my life. She predicted that it would take time for my attachment and bruising from Jon Rivers to work its way through my system, but in the end I would be able to wrap it up and box it off as something that occurred during a unique period of my life. She forecast that by May 2015, two of the rivers, health and work, would be flowing smoothly again. Her advice was to then just relax and enjoy the summer, and not to rush out and try to date, but to simply savor life again. I then thought about my beautiful garden, or getting out on the golf course again, or just being able to be with friends without them having to enquire about my health, and the anticipation of doing those activities made me smile. It would be life celebrated in the moment, and being with those who have tirelessly cheered me on in my journey. Her advice gave me a tremendous sense of peace.

Lesson learned: Ignore that inner voice at your peril. It speaks the truth.

HEALTH CHECK
January 26th, 2015

Despite all my current life challenges, my health is slowly but surely improving. I can feel myself returning back to normal life. My brain is coming back really strong, and the discharge from my drain is petering out, signaling that my time with an open drain and bandage changes is finally coming to a close. You will be glad to hear that my hair is a mass of 2-inch chemo curls and I have found the courage not wear a wig most of the time, if nothing else just to give my hair exposure to the air to grow. I personally do not like the new hairdo, but there are those who assure me, with hands over their heart, that they find my short curls rather charming and very much in vogue. But truth be known, I am just grateful that my hair is growing again at last; I never was a fan of being bald. I admire those people who can say "bald is beautiful," but I was never amongst them, and I feel more like my old self when I have my wig on.

However, I am still coping with some lymph node swelling and drainage, and neuropathy in my finger tips, which gives me fumble fingers, and of course the overwhelming fatigue. Last night I slept 11 hours, but I think it is stress that drives the fatigue, not breast cancer recovery. The business stress is such a meat grinder. But I tell myself that this too shall pass.

When all is said and done, I am profoundly grateful that my breast cancer side effects are receding at last. I can almost feel "normal." It has been a very long time coming. I can only liken it to a big storm that has raged with ferocity and now is passing through my body.

IN THE DOMAIN OF EVERYDAY MIRACLES
January 29th, 2015

I look at everyday miracles as those unexpected kindnesses from people or events that occur each and every day, if and when you pay attention.

For instance, last weekend I was attempting to load up my basket with ice melting crystal bags, which I had heard were still in stock at our local dollar store. The sales clerk, a woman in her 70s, saw me struggling and asked if she could help me. She told me to drive my car to the front of the store and she loaded the bags into the trunk. I wound down my window and told her that she was my angel for the day. Her face lit up and she thanked me. This was my first experience at a dollar store.

I make it my business to express my appreciation to all those along my path who show me unanticipated compassion or kindness. To me it is a little miracle, and I let them know that. There is such a lot of goodness in humanity when you tune into it. Everyday miracles are not life-altering and earth-shattering events, just the little kindnesses that people show you that make you smile. If you pay attention to them you will feel very blessed.

ON THE RAZOR'S EDGE
January 30th, 2015

As I have said before, this month I have been conducting a fire sale of my company. To say it is a stressful, exhausting, and at times a demoralizing experience doesn't even begin to capture what has been going on. Some of the proposed offers from suitors are enough to make my stomach churn, as they are like vultures circling, waiting for us to fall so they can feast on our bones. My staff are panicking as they see the company sliding and now barreling its way downhill. I have to be the fearless leader exuding calm, when in truth inside I am very anxious. Yet amongst it all, there are rays of hope and light. There are two or three better intentioned suitors, and one in particular whom I would actually be thrilled if they go through with the acquisition. It is a company that I have always felt would be a good match for us. This particular company's business and ours are a good strategic fit; they admire what we have accomplished, and they are large enough to help us grow and prosper again. And if we do, then so will I. I want to do right by our customers, vendors, and employees first and foremost. As for myself, that comes later. So I am fighting on and I hope to get some good news before the day is out. I truly need a boost right now.

I am aided and abetted by two wonderful women. My investment banker (broker), Claire, has been shielding me from some of the most anxiety provoking suitor conversations while keeping real prospects alive and well. God bless her, that is all I can say. Claire also referred me to a splendid woman lawyer, Christine, who told me that when this was all over I would be thankful that Jon Rivers resigned, because it forced my brain to wake up after its long sleep. She said that I would be much happier in the long run for it, and I was far from typical for my age, telling me that my brain was as alive as a 20 year old. I could have kissed her when she said that! She also said that when this was over, we could have dinner and it would be on her tab, because I clearly was a fascinating woman worth knowing better. When people say things like that when you are going through a tough time in life, they have no idea of how it can lift up your spirits and keep you going. Remember that when your friends are hurting.

When the day ended, I got the news that the CFO from my favorite prospective buyer will come to visit my company and meet with me and my staff for two days next week. He wants to get under the hood and examine whether we have a sustainable business. This is both encouraging and nerve-wracking at the same time. So much is riding on this. My anxiety is through the roof.

AS I LOOK FORWARD
February 1st, 2015

When I start looking to the future and ignore the anxiety of the present, my heart just leaps with joyful anticipation. I was talking to Debbie last night over dinner about her fledgling golfing skills. I have not been golfing for two years by this summer, and it will take time to get my game back, complicated by the fact that half my lymph nodes have been removed. But the idea of just golfing, not even keeping score, with such a good friend had me smiling in anticipation.

2014 was a year of almost complete social seclusion compared to my usual social Modus Operandi. I am not a happy-go-lucky extrovert who glad hands strangers at a party. In fact, I am rather shy. But I do enjoy connecting with people at an individual or small group level, and enjoying good conversation and laughter. I find that sort of social discourse very sustaining. I anticipate that new people will flow into my life; those that can accept that I am an intelligent, compassionate, working woman and allow me to be who I am without judgement. I know that I march to the beat of a different drummer than most women, let alone of my age, but I will welcome people into my life who can accept me the way I am.

I am really looking forward to getting this book published, my new blog and Facebook page underway, and my weekend speaking engagement circuit lifting off at last. I have been in front of audiences since being a university lecturer in Psychology at the University of Dundee at the grand old age of 23. I am a bit out of practice, but it is a part of my career that I always found enjoyable. I have much to say, stories to tell, and people to inspire to lead happier and healthier lives.

My sister Susan's words of wisdom still ring in my ears. I am not going to be in a rush to go out dating in 2015, although I'm open to anything happening more naturally in its own time. I can see that after Herman died, I wanted to fill that huge aching void in my life, and rushed out on a series of wildly unsuitable first dates. Then I had a 2-year platonic friendship with Jon. That showed me I was capable of deep intimacy with another man. But it also showed me what was missing and important to me, what I wanted and needed, above all else; a certain type of gentle kindness and unconditional acceptance of who I am. The greatest gift that Herman gave me was unconditional love. By being loved in such a profound way, it allowed me the fullest possibility for self expression. I want that again in my life. I am not so needy anymore and not in a hurry. That knowledge of myself is bringing me a sense of inner peace.

And lastly, but not the least, there is my day job at AllergyBuyers Club.com. I can truthfully say that, out of all the phases of my career, I have enjoyed it the most. I have derived great satisfaction from building a company, leading a team, and one that contributes so significantly to the health of others. Unexpectedly, I can see it will give me enormous satisfaction to help rebuild it and see it fly again. I thought I would just want to sell my company and be largely done with it. Now I am re-examining those assumptions. I have really enjoyed my conversations with the president of the company who is our lead prospective buyer. I think I could learn from him and enjoy working for him.

ON THE CUSP
February 7th, 2015

Today is one of those days where I have to exercise incredibly strong self control, as I am on the cusp between despair and hope for the future of my company. Discussions with various buyers have continued, but the options presented by most of them are, quite frankly, very distasteful. And now the CFO of the company that would be my first choice of financial backer of the company has some serious considerations about the financial risks involved in a turnaround investment and is not recommending to his boss that they proceed.

The deal is not quite dead yet, and discussions will continue all weekend, most of which will not include me until a decision has been made. And so I wait and I pray. I know I could deliver the results that this company needs. The question is whether I will be given the chance. I know rationally that worry is a useless emotion, and I need to face each next step as it is presented to me. But this is truly a rough challenge in self control. Forty-eight hours ago I was so optimistic. Now I am not nearly so sure, and that uncertainty is gnawing at me every hour of the day.

THE DISCUSSION RAGES
February 10th, 2015

For the past three days, discussions about the sale of my company have been going back and forth, including reams of data between us and the potential buyer. My emotions have been on a veritable roller coaster. It has been excruciating, knowing so many variables are at play before this potential buyer makes his final decision.

I know that I have given it my all, every single last ounce, far beyond what I knew was in me to give. And now I sit, wait, and pray. The alternatives to this deal not working out are completely horrendous, but I refuse to go there in my mind. I have fought with every fiber of my body, not only for myself, but for my employees, my customers, and my vendors. And if this all goes forward, as indeed I hope, I will praise God and thank my angels. I know that I could make this a win for the buyer. The suspense in this long wait has been as bad as when I paced the floor for four and a half hours while my husband had brain surgery. Both were, and have been, a battle for survival. I am so very tired.

MIRACLE IN THE MAKING
February 12th, 2015

As I have said before, there was only one company I wanted to acquire my business. One, I have thought over the years, with whom we could have a good synergistic business partnership. Tonight we got a draft agreement on the table. I know it will work. I get employment and the ability to do the right thing by my employees, my vendors, and my customers, and I get to walk proud and tall again. I trust that in time I will repair my damaged finances. It took practically every penny I had to prop the company up after the "financial mismanagement" a couple of years back. And then it was further compounded by well intentioned, but misguided management by Jon during his tenure as acting president. My senior staff are very proud of me, but I am just completely and utterly exhausted. It will be such a huge relief to have the legal documents actually signed and completed. It will also be satisfying to politely tell the vultures who have been hovering around waiting for us to fall so they could greedily pick over our bones, that they can now just take a hike.

Throughout this appalling nightmare of the last few weeks, I have been getting messages from Heaven to believe, to have faith, and this transaction will take place. I have asked the same question endlessly, desperately, and have kept getting the same answer. The answer has been that God loves me, and my husband, Herman, is protecting me from Heaven. I keep getting the message that my life is to be used for a higher purpose, which is why my life and my business are being spared.

I am very humbled, as I see the hand of the Divine at work. I think God chooses ordinary people to do extraordinary things. I see myself as very ordinary, but I know my life will gradually reveal the extraordinary. I am very clear that when this deal for acquiring my company is completed, it will be a major miracle and a direct intervention from above. As you may remember, my friends, I began this book in the quest to find my voice. I knew my voice had been muted, strangled by the tsunami of life-crippling events over recent years. Now I know that my voice is destined to be heard by millions, in service of a purpose higher than myself. I accept my destiny, and I am a humble servant of the something that has a context that is far greater than myself as an individual.

But in the meantime, I am waiting to sign this transaction to sell my company. We're not there yet. The wait is interminable. I am exhausted and could sleep for a week.

WAITING TO EXHALE
February 18th, 2015

These last few days have been an excruciating emotional marathon, where it has really been a matter of keeping the faith against all odds. I have been saying my prayers continuously throughout the day, and keep getting the answer that it will all turn out fine and not to worry. But I cannot help worrying. The rocks hurled at us at work seemed to have come fast and furious, as I have fought to keep the company out of bankruptcy and begged our creditors to be patient. Even though our potential buyer and I are well intentioned about coming to an agreement, nevertheless, serious impediments have presented themselves one after another, unbidden and unwanted. I have had to listen to meditation music at night to relax enough to get a few hours' sleep before dragging myself out of bed to go to work. I try very hard to dispense a bit of sunshine and optimism to my employees, but I know that I am wearing the stress all over my face. It is clear to them that I have been worried, very worried.

But tonight for the first time I am feeling a genuine sense of relief. It is like a gentle wave washing through my body, and I get to exhale at last. Maybe I will even get a normal night's sleep. Tomorrow I sign the "Letter of Intent" with the buyer to purchase our company. This is the first step towards final signature. Next week, a team of three people arrive from the buyer's headquarters to start helping us out of the ditch. And help cannot come too soon. We are in dire straits. But tonight I get to chill; just a little bit. We're nearly there.

STILL WAITING
February 28th, 2015

This last week was a whirlwind of working shoulder to shoulder with the team from the prospective buyer's company. The team were well received by my staff, who found them very smart but very pleasant to work with. It was a relief to find that they were not at all condescending. Together we fielded all the rocks and boulders that are being hurled at us by creditors, while all the time trying to get better margins from product vendors. It was exhilarating, exhausting, and very stressful, all at the same time. After they left, my team and I were left wondering, when will we get word that we are proceeding to contract? My staff gave 125% this week, as did I, and we are battle weary. We need a sign that there is light at the end of the tunnel. And so we still wait.

A GLASS OF WINE AND DESSERT
March 1st, 2015

I partake of wine and dessert rarely, but last night was an exception. Rose and I were out having dinner, having successfully navigated through the recent snowfall and ice on her driveway in this abysmal, record-breaking winter. I was ruminating and fretting about having heard no word as to whether my business transaction for acquisition was moving forward. I was not being the best of dinner companions. And then the news came: we are going to final contract.

A visceral wave of relief swept through me, and Rose and I celebrated quietly together. I can think of no better person to have witnessed the happy news. As we sat and talked, she, like others, reminded me that as my breast wound heals and spring comes, I will be outdoors again just enjoying nature and golfing again. I am very much aware that what is happening in my life is not what I envisaged a few years back. I could have sat all night talking about a bunch of "if onlys," starting with my husband's brain cancer six years ago. Back then, I was a wealthy woman and today I am not. But I see no value in pitying myself about how my life has changed so dramatically. There is only one way, and it is forward, and I need to trust in divine abundance to help me mend my finances and allow me to fulfill on my life's purpose.

The last few years of my life have been brutally hard. They have visibly aged me, humbled me, and tested me beyond all reasonable limits, but they have also given me infinite compassion for others, and I have gained hard earned wisdom about life. Would it be too much to pray that the tide is now finally turning in my favor? It would be such a gift to be able to look forward again and live a truly joyful life. I will never take it for granted.

THE FINAL PUSH
March 7th, 2015

My team and I have been working tirelessly to procure all the due diligence documents necessary for us to ink our business deal, while fending off creditors and designing a new spring catalog. The pace has been frenetic and we have had to keep tackling huge obstacles and accomplishing the impossible. It is like being in a road race while everyone is hurling boulders at you. I feel so sorry to have to put my staff through this. If only there was an easier way to get to the finish line. But we will get there.

THE NEXT CHAPTER
March 19th, 2015

My company was acquired this week. I wish I could say that I danced excitedly over the finish line amidst the cacophony of champagne corks popping, but it wasn't like that for me. Rather, it was more of a quiet acceptance that one glorious chapter of my life has ended. Clearly, this is not the way I envisaged it ending, as I am not the wealthy woman that I used to be. But, then, nothing in my life in recent years has been predictable or what I would have freely chosen. And yet, amidst it all, the confusion and the residue of the immense emotional pain from recent years, I have a deep faith that a new and great chapter in my life is about to begin. I am proud that, in choosing this buyer for my company, I have avoided formal bankruptcy and I am confident that my baby will grow to new heights, and my vendors, customers, and employees will all get fairly treated.

And then there is me. What am I doing next? I remain employed for as long as the new owners of the company want me around, and it makes me happy to be gainfully employed. I will spend my weekends spreading my message via my Facebook page and my inspirational blog, <u>OnlyOneLife.com</u>. My voice will now ring out its message "Only One Life: Don't Waste It" in my book and the Facebook page by the same name. I have found my voice and am whole again. I launched my blog publicly a few days ago and the Facebook page likes are pouring in. Local non-profits are already murmuring about having me speak at fundraisers. Speaking at a fundraising event at weekends will be far better than sitting at home bemoaning my fate as a widow.

I have rediscovered the woman who was so lost for so long, as she wandered aimlessly around in the wilderness. I can smile at my face in the mirror again. My life is just beginning its new chapter.

SPRING RISES

Like the weary pilgrim who places her dusty shoes at the shore,
Or the bloodied and bruised warrior princess who finally lays down her
sword,
I am nearing the end of my journey.
The winter was strewn with boulders of destruction along my path.
The wind of despair howled and shrieked in rage,
I kept relighting that flickering lantern of hope
Waiting for miracles to appear in the darkness,
And they did,
Raising me up when I had no more steps in me to take,
When my body screamed "no more!"
Loving friends who believed that spring would arrive
Gave me courage to take those last faltering steps.
Slaying the last dragons of misery which threatened to consume me with
their greedy open jaws.
Peace. Silence.
My heart is full of gratitude as I look out the window,
The spring flowers are bravely pushing their heads through the hard and
frozen ground
Eager for the summer warmth to arrive.
The cocoon will break open and the butterfly will fly free again

Mercia Tapping

SPONSORS

If you would like to help sponsor me in my work spreading the word through my blog "Only One Life," plus the Facebook page and speaking engagements of "Only One Life: Don't Waste It," and also help me retire the personal debts that followed me after the sale of my company, I would be deeply grateful. You can send it as a tax free gift up to $14K per individual and $28K per couple each calendar year. The address to send it to is:

Mercia Jane Tapping,
Only One Life,
74 Benjamin's Gate,
Plymouth, MA 02360.

I thank you from the bottom of my heart. I believe in miracles.

RESOURCES AND MORE

1. The best source of information about breast cancer that I have found is <u>BreastCancer.org</u>

2. A charity for brain cancer awareness and research for a cure is The Dragon Master Foundation. It was founded by Amanda Haddock, a friend of mine. <u>dragonmasterfoundation.org</u>

3. GBM & Brain Cancer Warrior Women is the secret group I belong to on Facebook for women who are caregivers or have lost a loved one to brain cancer. It is a secret group and you will need to friend me on my personal page, Mercia Jane Tapping on Facebook, and then you can be added to the group.

4. If you have allergies, asthma, or sinus issues, or just want to create a healthy home, please visit <u>AllergyBuyersClub.com</u>

5. <u>GrayRibbonFunding.com</u> has a wonderful collection of recipes contributed by the brain cancer community to fundraise for a cure.

6. My book cover was courtesy of <u>selfpubbookcovers.com</u> and the artist was Daniela. I think she did an awesome job.

7. Jon Rivers is a pseudonym and not his real name. I think you can understand why I did not reveal his name. It protects both our privacy, and he is a very private man.

8. Claire Gruppo of <u>glconline.com</u> is a senior partner of Gruppo, Levy and Co. out of NYC. She is an investment banker and I could not recommend her more strongly if you need someone to represent you to conduct the sale of a company. She produced rabbits out of hats and kept the sale of my company alive when lesser mortals would have given up.

KEEP IN TOUCH

If you wish to find out when I achieve the life of my successful twin, you can follow me on Facebook under Mercia Jane Tapping. If you want to continue to be inspired by my writing and philosophy of life, please follow OnlyOneLife.com, the blog, or "Only One Life; Don't Waste It" on Facebook.

I am available to speak at non-profit organizations at low or no charge, within 75 miles of my house in Plymouth, MA. I speak on several main themes: "Daily Miracles," "Only One Life: Don't Waste It," and "Thriving, Not Just Surviving, When Faced With A Major Illness." I can speak to other themes on special request. I generally charge for speaking at non-profits further afield unless my funds permit otherwise. I also charge professional speaking rates for profit-based companies. You can email me through Facebook or my blog for a discussion of rates. I have a lifetime of experience in public speaking. I speak from the heart and with a dry wit that accompanies my British accent. I love what I do and am very good at it because I am passionate about making a difference in the lives of my audience, and that comes across in my speaking.